WOODCOCK & SON
BOOT MAKERS

CW00585116

The Warming Stone

Reminiscences of
early 20th Century childhood
in Chapel-en-le-Frith,
Derbyshire

by
ADA HITCHENS

Chapel-en-le-Frith, Derbyshire, England SK23 9RQ
ISB 0947848 16 9

ISBN 0947848 16 9

Reprinted 1999

The Warming Stone,
published by Caron Publications,
a division of The Peak Press Company, of Chapel-en-le-Frith,
as a celebration of the Millennium
and as a contribution to the
recorded social history of Chapel-en-le-Frith and Derbyshire.

Typeset, designed and printed in England by The Peak Press Company,
Chapel-en-le-Frith, High Peak, Derbyshire, SK23 9RQ.

Front cover taken from a painting by the author Ada Hitchens.
End papers: Front, The Market Place, Coronation celebrations, King George V, June 22, 1911.
Back, The Market Place, Coronation celebrations, King George VI, May 12, 1937.

Graphic design and additional illustrations by Claire Liversidge

Dedicated to the memory of my sister Winnie.
Together we shared these experiences.

Chapel Rose Queen 1912
(Winnie, second from left)

Acknowledgements

My thanks to Robert Mulholland, editor and publisher, of Caron Publications, and to The Peak Press Company, for their skill, encouragement and understanding in the production of this book and particularly to Claire Liversidge for the design and to Marion Rowbotham for the use of photographs of her late father, F. B. Hills. My friends Dorothy Stewart and Ann Marchington were a great encouragement to me while I was writing the book and gave generously of their time. My niece Mrs Clare Mortin has also been a great support and has helped me particularly by carefully checking proofs. To these people and the many others who have helped along the way, I wish to express my gratitude.

Ada Hitchens, *Chapel-en-le-Frith, January 1998.*

Photographs

Most of the photographs used in the book are from the collection taken by the late Mr F. B. Hills. A number of other photographs are from the private collections of Mrs Jean Bailey, Mrs Alwin Carrington, Mrs Jennifer Mulholland and Ferodo Limited. Efforts have been made to trace and acknowledge the ownership of others and we apologise for any unintentional breach of copyright.

Contents

Introduction		6
Chapter One	Not a Pretty Place	10
Chapter Two	The Last Days of the Working Horse	18
Chapter Three	The Rhythm of Life	26
Chapter Four	The Warming Stone	37
Chapter Five	Where have all the Trees Gone?	49
Chapter Six	Local Characters	52
Chapter Seven	The Working Week	70
Chapter Eight	Neighbours	88
Chapter Nine	The Inns of the Market Place	94
Chapter Ten	The Local Shops	99
Chapter Eleven	Starting School	105
Chapter Twelve	When Winter Came	111
Chapter Thirteen	Health and Hygiene	115
Chapter Fourteen	The Building of the Viaduct	122
Chapter Fifteen	Sights and Sounds of Wakes Week	130
Chapter Sixteen	A Midsummer Day's Dream	134
Chapter Seventeen	The Beginning of the End	140
Index		143-144

INTRODUCTION

Once upon a time, shopping in Chapel-en-le-Frith was a pleasant experience. I just took my time, stopping to chat with a friend or two I might meet along the way, or enjoying looking at the displays in shop windows. In the shops I was graciously served by either the owner or his assistant. If I wished, instead of carrying a heavy load, I could leave an order and it would be delivered to my home later in the day.

Now, all that has changed and shopping can only be described as a traumatic experience. The pounding and roar of the traffic make it impossible to try to hold a conversation with anyone. All I can do is smile wanly and hurry on before being either shaken off the pavement or splashed with mud from a heavy vehicle passing by.

Every door and window is besmirched with mud which makes the street a depressing sight as I wend my way home. I walk down Rowton Road and reach the sanctuary of the Park. It looks serene and well maintained, its natural beauty left undisturbed, just as Chapel used to be in my young days.

I sit on a seat for a while and my mind drifts back to the Chapel I knew and loved when I was a child, more than eighty years ago. I reason that, sensibly, there was bound to be change with progress, especially after two World Wars. I realise how fortunate I was to have lived in Chapel all those years ago, and to have enjoyed such a full yet simple life.

I was living in Tunstead Milton when I decided to write my memoirs of childhood days in Chapel-en-le-Frith. My young neighbour Valerie Hill became interested and offered to type my handwritten pages. I am most grateful for her encouragement and all the help she gave me. Eventually I left Tunstead and went to live again in the centre of Chapel. This disrupted my writing for a considerable time. I was eighty-four years old when I decided to continue with it. My eyesight had deteriorated badly and I would have given up had it not been for two friends, Dorothy Stewart and Ann Marchington, who insisted that I carried on with it. So, with much enlarged letters on a typewriter, I proceeded. Over the next two years with great patience they gave most generously of their time and knowledge. I can never thank them enough. We were almost sorry when the story was eventually told! I only hope anyone who might read this will get as much pleasure and fun from it as we had producing it.

I have called my story THE WARMING STONE because it was the hub of our childhood pleasures. The "warming stone" was a solid slab of gritstone that formed the flat roof of a low boiler house of the brewery in Park Road in the centre of Chapel. The brewery has long gone but it was once located adjacent to the Memorial Institute, the popular working men's club.

At the end of a brewing session, the stone slab was warm enough for me and my friends to sit upon, sheltered from the wind and the cold. Huddled together, we would play our childish games, word games and the like, sometimes telling ghost stories until our parents came to tell us it was bedtime. For me, that solid slab of Derbyshire Gritstone with its strength and warmth epitomised the quality of life enjoyed by the people of Chapel-en-le-Frith.

The first thing that I can positively remember is of a warm summer day and I was sitting on the shallow stone step of the porch that sheltered our front door on the main street, Market Street. I had just had a treat.

A boy called Erbie Ford, who lived down the street, had come to take me to see the new pigeon loft his parents had bought him for his birthday. I held his hand as we walked down the street. I was a bit frightened. It was so quiet. The only sound was of our footsteps on the pavement. We went into the garden at the back of the house where his parents were admiring the new loft. The pigeons were restless in their new home and their fluttering and strutting frightened me. I cried, so they took me into the house and gave me a biscuit.

Later, Erbie came into the house carrying two pigeons by their legs. They were limp as he put them on the floor and they twitched. Erbie wasn't looking very happy as his mother said: "We are having pigeon pie for our dinner tomorrow love". I cried again, so Erbie put something into my pocket and took me home.

My mother came out of the house and sat me on the step again. That is how I came to be sitting there, exploring the warm smooth thing that Erbie had put into my pocket. My mother asked what I had and when I showed her she said "It's a pigeon's egg. What a blessing you did not break it. You would have been in an awful mess".

Ada as an infant: The first thing that I can possibly remember...

That was the day I discovered the menace of eggs and became interested in the street and curious about the things that were happening around me. What I learned and saw that day set the pattern for my young life. I would be about three years old at the time.

My sister Winnie and I were born in a cottage on Market Street opposite what is now Thornbrook Road and where the Drill Hall used to stand.

When my grandfather died, we moved into the family house which was still on Market Street but opposite the Town Hall. I lived there until 1939, during which time there was the first World War

A resident of Combs, Herbert Frood (inset) founder of Ferodo Ltd., transferred his business activities from Mancheser in 1902 to Sovereign Mill, a former textile warehouse on Hayfield Road.

and a way of life began to change.

Cars had been invented and a newcomer to Chapel called Herbert Frood, who lived in Combs and worked in an old mill with a water wheel, invented a brake lining for cars. He started to produce these in an old mill at the bottom of Hayfield Road. There was a large house attached to it which he used as an office. His product was a success and eventually became world famous.

From then on, Chapel changed dramatically and a way of life was ended.

CHAPTER ~ 1 ~

NOT A PRETTY PLACE

I cannot say that Chapel was ever a pretty place. It had no cottage gardens or village green to enhance it, but the houses, built substantially of sandstone, blended beautifully into the landscape of hills and moorland which surrounded Chapel. It was wholesome and unpretentious as were the people who lived in it. They were generous and warm-hearted and true to the Derbyshire character, bestowed with a great sense of humour.

There was no real poverty in Chapel. Work could be found locally for almost everyone. At Lingards or Smithfield Wadding Work, the Town End Foundry, Ibbotsons Engineering Works, the Shirt works and the Gas Works. Maids, gardeners, grooms were employed at the big houses and estates such as Ford Hall and The Ridge - and Bowden Hall employed caretakers, chauffeurs and cleaners. Plenty of casual labour was available and a lot of men were employed in the building trade, where there was always work for stone-masons, plumbers, joiners. A substantial number of men worked in the limestone quarries at either Dove Holes or Peak Dale and many were employed on the two railway lines. With steady wages coming into most homes, there was a relaxed and confident atmosphere in the town.

Chapel was always clean and tidy. The street was swept by the Council every week and people took pride in seeing that the stone slab pavements were swilled every Friday night. This was almost a ritual. At every house after tea-time, husbands and wives would be carrying buckets of water out and scrubbing away with a broom. As a finishing touch, the door step would be washed and yellow-stoned then finished off with a band of white stone along the edge.

There was keen competition, particularly among the women, as to who had the cleanest house or who was the best cook. In spite of this, there was a friendly atmosphere and if

A relaxed and confident atmosphere in the town...
Market Street at Town End

anyone was in trouble, neighbours would rally round to give what help they could.

It was not easy in those days to keep houses clean. One reason was that the roads were not coated with tarmacadam but with limestone rubble. In dry and windy weather the soft surface of the road blew up in dust and got into the houses through open windows or doors. When the weather was wet, the surface of the road became slurry. This was trampled into the houses and needed constant cleaning off the floors.

In wet weather, a strange looking vehicle went up and down the street. It was, of course, horse-drawn and shaped like a long barrel. It had an opening half way up which was the full width of the container. Under this was a long round brush which was set at an angle sloping towards the gutter. As the vehicle moved, the brush turned and swept the slurry to the side of the road. Every few yards the horse stopped and the man in charge shovelled the slurry into the container. When full, this was taken to the Council tip and emptied.

The wear and tear of the traffic soon wore the surface away which then needed replacing. Consequently, the road built up higher and higher until it became a rounded shape on top, falling quite steeply into the gutters. The hill became steeper, which made it hard work for the horses pulling heavy loads.

It remained like this until electricity came to Chapel in the late 1920s. The centre of the road was then dug out to lay the cables. At the same time the road surface was lowered, then tarred and gravelled. This was done by spraying the road with hot tar, then Council workers covered it with gravel, carried by the spadeful from heaps at the side of the road. This made it particularly difficult to cross the street for a few days as the tar remained soft and runny.

It was an exciting time for the children (and plenty of grown-ups) when the steam roller was brought in to flatten gravel and tar. It was a splendid machine! Huge and beautiful to look at. It was always beautifully cared for by the driver. There was a brass horse mascot on the front always bright and shining. The steam roller was usually kept near to the work in

Hearse House (right) now the Heritage Centre and George Taylor's milk float.

hand. The driver slept in the wooden caravan next to it, so that it would be stoked up and ready for off early in the morning.

Adding to the good appearance of the street were the neat stone walls and decorative railings at the front of the two churches and Town Hall. The entrance to the Town Hall was quite impressive, with huge wrought iron gates leading to the broad shallow steps up to the front doors. This looked especially so on Court days.

In those days, Chapel really was the Capital of the Peak. Criminal charges in the Peak were tried on Court days in the Town Hall. The Court was held on the third Thursday on the month. Chapel came alive on that day. The street was busy with spectators, reporters, caterers. High-ranking police in their uniforms made an impressive sight. There was always a stir in the spectators when the defendants arrived, especially if they were local.

I have praised the cleanliness of the street, but I must admit to a detriment which we accepted as an every day occurrence which could not be avoided. All traffic was horse-drawn in my early days and at certain times each day (especially when the farmers were taking their milk to the station twice a day) there were piles of horse manure on the road. This was soon spread by cartwheels. Carts were also left outside shops and there were usually several waiting at the corn shop. This meant that the horses often urinated, which ran down the gutters. Particularly in hot weather this pollution stank. The Council employed men as street cleaners to remove the horse droppings with shovels and a bin on two wheels.

This pollution attracted hoards of flies which pervaded the houses and shops. Fly papers hanging from beams or gas lights were the usual method of catching some of them. These were long strips of paper with very sticky glue on both sides. Flies settled on them and were caught. The papers were soon covered and then they were cut down and burnt. However, there always seemed to be those who escaped and at night the ceiling would be well dotted with them resting till daylight.

It is almost impossible to believe that in those days there were no such things as plastic bags or dustbins, let alone wheelie bins to collect household rubbish in. Instead, in the yard at the back of each cottage, one small part was walled off to make a square shape. All household refuse was thrown into this space. The theory was that the ashes taken each day from the kitchen fire grate helped to bury the objectionable and smelly things which were thrown in the ashpit.

It was not so bad in Winter but in the heat of Summer there was always a stench from it. Naturally, this attracted lots of flies, particularly bluebottles. When there was a large amount in the pit, a horse and cart was brought into the yard and the refuse was shovelled into the cart and taken to the tip. The pit was then hosed down and ready to be filled again. There were no laws on hygiene and so many diseases must have been spread by all the flies.

Milk was served from a churn which more often than not had been standing in the farmyard with just a piece of muslin tied onto the top to sieve the milk as it was poured from the bucket used to milk the cow. There was dust galore and cow droppings in the shippons which must have polluted it.

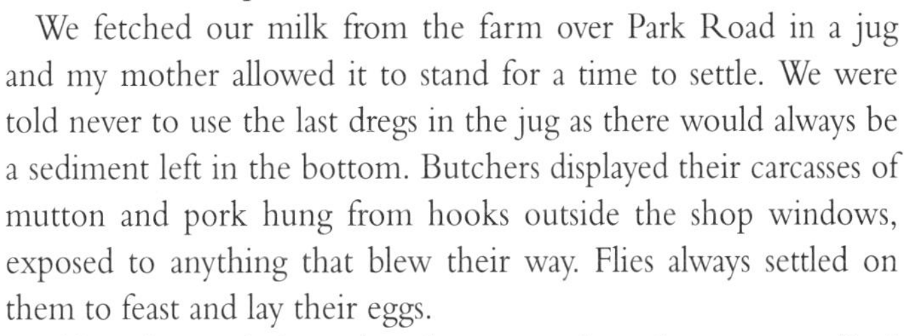

We fetched our milk from the farm over Park Road in a jug and my mother allowed it to stand for a time to settle. We were told never to use the last dregs in the jug as there would always be a sediment left in the bottom. Butchers displayed their carcasses of mutton and pork hung from hooks outside the shop windows, exposed to anything that blew their way. Flies always settled on them to feast and lay their eggs.

Although people kept their houses so clean they never realised the danger they were in from contaminated foods. All cooking and heating of houses was from a coal fire. Very comforting to sit before and there was no better way of cooking to retain the flavour of food.

The price to be paid was smell from the smoke which came from every chimney in the town. One could almost set your clock by the smoke coming out of the chimneys as wives stoked up to cook a meal for the family coming home from work.

From the top of the hill, one could see all the chimneys exuding smoke. On windless days it came out tall and straight, then people would smile and say that it meant fine weather was to come, but if the weather was stormy, the smoke hardly left the chimney before it was battered by the wind down onto the street, making your eyes sore and giving you a smarting chest.

Sometimes in the houses, the smoke could not get away up the chimney and was blown back into the room. This was horrible and meant that doors and windows had to be left open for the smoke to be drawn out of the house. This accounted for so many people suffering from bronchitis.

It was a common sight to see a chimney on fire. This was caused when a chimney needed sweeping and the soot ignited from a very high flame. It was often a spectacular sight with flames and sparks like a firework display and billowing black smoke blown by the wind in all directions. Neighbours would be dashing to close their doors and windows to keep the smoke out.

Fortunately, things would progress. Few people have coal fires today and the bronchitis they caused would soon be all but banished.

Ironically, these days were a part of the everyday way of life that I really loved. In the years to come, change would be all around. And, sadly, change meant that the days of the working horse were also numbered…

The working horse:
Their days were numbered…

CHAPTER ~ 2 ~

THE LAST DAYS OF THE WORKING HORSE

It is difficult to believe that for a great part of the day the street would be almost silent. Possibly just the sound of a cock crowing over at Longson's Farm, answered by one at Frith's down the road, or the Church clock striking and chiming the hour. Possibly the sound of a train in the distance puffing up the line to Dove Holes Tunnel or a horse and cart being backed under the archway at the corn shop, then a dull thud as a bag of corn was dropped through a trap door into the cart below.

Every mid-day, except Sunday, the Church bell would be rung for five minutes. This was an ancient custom to call the people in for their dinner break. This custom has been carried on and most places of work had a break from twelve till one. At the mills, the workforce was called back to work by a hooter at one o'clock.

After the crowing of the cocks in the early morning, the next sound that stirred you into getting out of bed would be the sound of Sam Slack and Paddy Muir wearing their heavy working boots, going over the road opposite our house to feed the horses at John Arthur Garlick's stable. J.A. Garlick was a furniture remover and these two men were his workforce. This usually coincided with the men who walked every day to work in the quarries at Dove Holes.

They each carried a straw container slung over their shoulder. This in Derbyshire was called a 'bass'. It contained their food for the day, including tea and sugar for a brew up, and more likely than not precious tools they had made themselves in the forge at the quarry.

Across the road from our house, Mr. Walker opened his shop about then and the paper boys brought the papers from the station to be sorted and delivered to customers in the village. At the same time with the postman delivered the mail.

A beautiful view of Chapel-en-le-Frith from the North West Station. These fields are practically all built on now.

The street would now begin to get busy with people drifting towards their place of work. The late ones hurrying to be there before the factory hooter sounded. Although these hooters summoned the people to work there was nothing aggressive about them until the Second World War when they were no longer used to summon people to work but to alert people that an air raid was imminent. Then they were blown at full blast for about five minutes and all the A.R.P. services went on alert. It was a great relief when they were blown again as an All Clear signal.

At about a quarter to nine, the children would be on their way to school passing up and down the street; some to the Wesleyan School in Town End, the others to the Church School on High Street. All the children had to walk as there was no transport as there is today. Some had to walk to and from school as far away as Whitehough or Sparrowpit..

After nine o'clock when the children were in school, the street was quiet for a time, and housewives and shopkeepers were busy sweeping and tidying the pavements.

Now began quite a busy time as the farmers came in their floats to take their milk to the station to be put on the train to Manchester. The floats were taken up Station Road and tethered to the railings, then the churns of milk were lifted out of the float and manhandled across the level crossing onto the Manchester line.

The horses could be left as they were so used to the noise of the train that they accepted it, with the exception of one which belonged to Jonathan Smith from Slack Hall Farm.

It was said that he never broke his horses in!

During the school holidays we were told to play in our yard until the farmers had returned from the station, as Jonathan Smith's horse was bound to run away.

We used to wait with excitement and we were rarely disappointed at the spectacle of the horse roaring down the street with Jonathan standing in the float like a Roman charioteer.

Jonathan was an unorthodox farmer. He had a bull which was known to be savage. It had a ring through its nose for a leading pole but Jonathan did not have one. Instead he used an old umbrella. The bull just tossed his head, broke the umbrella and gored Jonathan. He was very badly hurt. I could go on for a long time telling stories about Slack Hall Farm.

A large handcart loaded with sides of beef was trundled to the station and over the level crossing to be put on the train to Manchester and delivered to a well-known restaurant called "Parkers".

All this hustle of loading the train was done by porters and watched over by the Station Master, Mr. Dawe, who wore a smart uniform and a hat trimmed with gold braid which he touched with respect as travellers came onto the station. The porters also opened and closed carriage doors for you.

Every day about this time, the tramps who had had a night's lodging in the workhouse would be coming down the street on their way to the next haven, which would be at Bakewell Workhouse. They were given food and a bed, then in the morning some work would be found for them to do before they set out on their wanderings again. Each night these men would be coming up the street about five o'clock. They knew the trail well, and we often watched them looking at the walls to find a hole in which to hide their treasures as they did not want to have to disclose these to the Workhouse master. In the morning they would collect them as they went on their way. They all walked in the gutter with eyes down looking for cigarette ends that had been thrown away.

There would be a lull in the street for a time, then up the street from Park Farm would be Tom Longson delivering milk and at the same time down the street came Walter Barlow also delivering milk from door to door.

As the two floats drew level, people would stop on the street or come to their door to listen to the banter that passed between the two men.

There would pass a dialogue between them that was never bettered by any stand up comic on stage. Although it was always at the other's expense there was never any offence taken. They just continued on ladling the milk out of the churn into the can for the customers.

I cannot pass on without mentioning Tom Longson's horse Maggie. She was a quiet little skewbald pony who never had to be driven. She knew every house where milk had to be delivered and just moved on her own as Tom stopped and chatted to people he knew.

He never knew her origin, he bought her off a gypsy, but one day a strange thing happened to me. I was walking past a little croft where Maggie was grazing. On that day there was a parade coming up the street headed by the Town Band. They were playing a lively march and as I looked at Maggie, she lifted her head and appeared to be listening. Then suddenly, she started to dance two steps to the left and then right, then she turned in a circle. This was in absolute time to the band. She went round and round and, as she got in front of me, the band stopped and she went down on one knee and bowed.

This proved that at some time in her life she must have been in a circus and she remembered performing to the music of a band all those years before.

Next to our house, 36 Market Street, is the old Primitive Methodist Chapel (now John Kelly's joiner's workshop). It belonged to my grandfather who bought it when the Chapel moved into the new building across the road. When my grandfather died my father let it as a store room to

My clay models of the farmers who added so much to Chapel life. They are (from left): Standing at rear: Walter Barlow, Down Lee Farm, and Tom Longson, Park Farm; Front: Jodie Berrisford, Lower Courses Farm and Isaac Nadin, Bowden Head Farm, with a gentleman farmer on his weekly visit to Chapel cattle market.

John Arthur Garlick who was a furniture remover.

My sister and I were often awakened in the early hours of the morning by Sam Slack and Paddy Muir harnessing their horses to the large van to take a load away. Everything was done as quietly as possible so as not to disturb people from their sleep. More often than not Winnie and I would get out of bed to watch the operation.

The horses were always spoken to very quietly and gently. Paddy and Sam loved their horses dearly. Paddy looked after Punch, a big grey horse, whilst Sam cared for the brown horse called Charlie.

Paddy would sometimes get irritated when Punch was not doing as he wished. He would swear in a soft voice and run at him as if he was going to kick him, then he would just stand and stamp his feet. Old Punch would look at him with a bored yet reproving look. Then Paddy would put his hand on Punch's head and pat him. There was great understanding between them.

I think one of the saddest things I ever saw in my young life was when Mr. Garlick turned to motor transport and the horses had to go. It was very early one morning, just after dawn, when my mother woke us to see the horses depart. Their new owners were waiting in the street by our house as the horses were brought from the stable, Paddy and Mr. Slack leading them. I don't know where they were going but it was too far for us ever to see them again.

Both men put their arms around their horses neck and patted and patted them. The horses knew there was something wrong, and were restless. At last the men moved off with them and Paddy and Mr. Slack stood in the middle of the road watching until they were out of sight. Punch kept turning round trying to come back again. By this time Paddy was sobbing and when they had gone he leaned against our house wall and cried as if heartbroken.

My father always said he was never the same again. He was a bachelor and lived alone. Punch must have been his whole life.

The Market Place on market day…a busy day, with farmers in floats and groups standing in the street talking or bargaining.

CHAPTER ~ 3 ~

THE RHYTHM OF LIFE

There was a rhythm to the way of life in the town each week until Saturday at twelve noon. One could say that the rhythm was also broken on Thursdays which was market day, when farmers brought their cattle into the town to sell or to buy more stock.

This was certainly a busy day, with farmers in floats and groups standing in the street talking or bargaining. The cattle for sale had been driven in, not transported in trucks as they are today. They came in from each end of the town and along with horses and floats converged on the Market Place, which was bigger in those days. The street was narrower and the Market Place came as far as the street without footpaths. There were two flights of steps going up straight from the road. There was no War Memorial but a square shape of stone steps with a wrought iron lamp stand called the Lily ground and a trough with water which must have been a Godsend to the thirsty cattle which had probably been driven several miles to the market.

The horses would be tethered to the railings, given a nose bag of corn and left to their own devices, more often than not dozing off to sleep.

There would be groups of farmers in the market or street laughing and talking, then slapping each others hands as they struck a bargain. This signified a deal had been struck. After that, no-one would go back on it. A farmer's word, once given, was his bond. Sometimes the market would be full and all down the street there would be groups of farmers and cattle. This made it hazardous if you had to go out to the shops.

I think market day was an important day out for the farmers. There was so much greeting of friends and relatives. My mother always had a busy time on Thursdays as most of her relatives were local farmers and they all called in for a chat and a cup of tea.

My mother's cousin Clara, who lived at Bowden Head Farm, brought home-made butter for sale. Each farm who churned butter had their own butter stamp. Bowden Head's stamp was a round shape with roses and leaves. Clara carried it in a long flat basket lined with wet muslin cloth in the summertime. Then on very hot days she cut rhubarb leaves out of the garden and put them in layers over the muslin cover on the butter to keep it cool.

Public houses did a roaring trade and at the end of the day many a horse used to find its own way home with a clapped out farmer asleep in the bottom of the float.

There were various activities during the week. Some regular and other vendors who were regular visitors but not a weekly service.

Mr. Partridge, who kept a greengrocers shop in the Market Place, came down the street every Tuesday, shouting for trade. On hearing him people would come out of their houses and stand around the cart chatting to each other. As well as fruit and vegetables, he had a flap at the back of the cart which was filled with boxes of fish. There were no fish shops in Chapel and this was a chance to buy cod, hake, herrings and kippers. In season there would be two sacks hanging at the back of the cart filled with cockles and mussels. These were sold by the quart and were very popular and cheap. My mother used to buy the cockles which had to be well rinsed to get rid of as much sand as possible, then she would put them in a huge pan to boil.

We were then given the job of flicking the cockle out of the shell into a dish. We could not do this fast enough, then scoop up the shells to take into the garden to find a place to decorate with them. I don't think there was a garden in the town that did not boast a cockle shell pattern.

Another regular was a tall slim man who would be seen coming down the street at a brisk pace on Monday mornings. He was called Reuben Bennet and he sold yeast to confectioners

The Market Place, around 1940, long after alterations had been made to make room for motor vehicles on the main road. Note the lovely flower beds outside the Roebuck Inn.

and grocers shops. He carried this in two large bundles wrapped in blue and white cloth. These were tied together and slung over his shoulder. Each bundle was about as big as a football. They were put on the counter in the shop then the grocer stated how much he wanted and it was cut off and weighed.

There was no delivery of bread from larger bakeries in those days. Everybody baked their own and yeast for it was bought from the grocer. I used to love the taste of yeast and always tried to steal a bit. Mothers used to give their children yeast to eat sometimes as it was supposed to be a cure for worms.

There was also another use for yeast. We used to go with my mother into the croft at the back of our house to gather nettles to make nettle beer. We would take a clothes basket to carry them in as you needed a good many. Needless to say, we got stung and most of our time was spent in finding dock leaves to rub them with to ease the pain.

The nettles were washed then put into a jam pan with water and sugar. This was boiled for quite a time then the liquid was poured off into a pansion. A slice of bread was toasted, covered with a thick layer of yeast, and floated on top of the liquid for hours.

The yeast melted on the toast and fermented the beer. Bottles were then filled and corked - never with a screw top as the beer became very active and blew the corks off. After a few days it was mature and drinkable. I still think it was the most delicious drink ever made.

Another welcome sight on the street was the rag and bone man. People saved scraps of cloth and old clothes to exchange with him for either a few coppers or pieces of yellow or white stone to clean and decorate their steps.

The yellow stone was round and hard, being a natural stone but the white was square, smooth and soft. It was manufactured, possibly from fire clay. It had a donkey imprinted on it and was always known as donkey stone. This was used as a line of decoration on the edge of a step after it had been washed and yellow stoned.

Another thing he sold was large blocks of salt from the salt mines in Cheshire. They were about two feet long and six inches square. My mother used to buy these and after scraping all the outside off to be sure it was clean, we children were given the job of scraping it onto a board then storing it in a jar until needed.

Whenever Mr. Hallam from Eaves Farm killed a pig, my father used to buy a side of bacon from him, also a ham. Most of the salt would then be used to preserve the flesh. We had a large stone bench in the pantry and the ham and bacon were put on it, then salt was rubbed into them every day until they were considered cured. They were then hung from the ceiling on large hooks and slices were cut off when needed.

Another welcome trader was Mr. Beardwood who sold flappy oatcakes. They were made from oatmeal and were a Derbyshire speciality. When toasted and buttered they were lovely but most people fried them with their bacon in the morning and then they were both delicious and nourishing.

Periodically on the street would be seen two men wheeling what looked like a large coffer and I suppose that is what it really was. Although there was no electricity in those days, most people had gas. No bills were sent out to pay for it but each house had a slot meter into which you put coins whenever the gas pressure began to fall. Every few weeks the two men, one called Arthur Barlow and the other one Mr. Taylor, called at houses to empty the money from the meter. This was carried away in the contraption on wheels.

Occasionally a welcome sight for housewives would be a man trundling a strange looking machine, again on wheels. It had a treadle that turned a stone wheel. He sharpened knives and scissors. People would queue up for this service as most wives did all the sewing needed in the home plus cutting up old coats etc. into long strips, then into small pieces to peg into hessian to make hearth rugs during the Winter nights.

Another most unusual vendor was a short stocky Jew who used to come about once a year selling sheet music. He carried a large flat carrier on his back and was a strange sight in the street. He did a fair trade as many families owned either a piano or some other musical instrument. This may seem strange but in those days there was no television or radio. Entertainment was made in your own home and occasionally a concert was given in the town with local talent. There were no shops selling sheet music and this was a much appreciated service.

There is one other vendor I must not forget to mention. She was Maggie Brunt who hawked home-made teacakes from door to door most days of the week. She lived with her two sisters, Polly and Ann in a cottage near Ibbotson's Mill, which was situated on the main street in Town End by Smith Brook. They baked bread and teacakes for a living. They were all short and plump and Ann was stooped and round shouldered from a lifetime of bending over a pansion, kneading bread and putting it into the oven, which was a side oven to a Yorkshire range. It burned coal and it must have been hard work stoking it and keeping the right temperature for the bread.

They managed to make a living out of it with Polly working at the vicarage to help Mrs. Streader, the Vicar's wife. People went to the house to buy the bread, which was delicious and Maggie hawked the teacakes round the houses.

The three sisters lived a very simple, almost empty life, going to church twice on Sundays and attending church functions was the highlight of their lives. The exception was that they relished all the gossip Maggie picked up as she went from house to house. She was a master at wheedling news and bits of scandal from people.

She would knock on the door then lift the latch, open it a little way, then calling "Do you want any today Mrs. Bramwell?" at the same time worming her way into the room. She would then put the long shallow basket on the table displaying her delicious looking and smelling teacakes which no one could resist. Then, whilst the money was being exchanged

Simpson's Butchers shop. Shopping was made easy because everybody knew each other.

she would begin "Have you heard about so and so? They tell me such and such. Do you know if it is true or not?" My mother would answer with her mind possibly on something cooking in the oven "I really don't know Maggie. There have been rumours going about". Then realising that my mother was not going to say any more Maggie, well satisfied that there must be something going on, was away to gather more information at the next house.

By the time she got home she would have the whole story to pass on to her sisters. They knew so much about the local tittle-tattle that they could have written a book. When I was sent for a loaf to the house, I was told by my mother not to tell them anything, which was not easy as I sat on their sofa in that warm room with the delicious smell of baking bread. You almost answered their questions in a dream.

Some of the butchers shops had primitive freezers like a large cupboard. Ice was delivered in blocks by men who carried it with long iron grapples so as not to freeze their hands.

Beer was delivered to the inns from the breweries by horse and dray. Once I remember two horses coming loaded with barrels when one horse took fright at the top of the hill. It bolted and the second horse was sliding behind with sparks going up from its shoes like bonfire night. The barrels rolled off the lorry and bounced down the road. People ran in all directions to save injury. One lady was standing on a stool cleaning her windows when a barrel went onto the pavement and missed her by inches.

Apart from the farmers going to take milk to the station there was no constant flow of traffic. Everybody had a coal fire so there was more often than not a coal lorry delivering bags of coal to houses in the street.

Late on Saturday afternoons it would be no unusual sight to see the strange figure of a man moving from place to place in the street. He was dressed in black knee breeches and a green jacket with a short cape and a tricorn hat on his head. He carried a hand bell which he rang as he moved from place to place. He was the Town Crier and after shouting "O Yeah" a few times he would, in a loud voice, announce any coming events in the next week, such as sales, concerts or sports events. There was no local paper and this was a good way of advertising as everybody stopped to listen. The bell in later years was used to announce the closing of the Memorial Park every night.

Shopping was made easy by the fact that everybody knew each other and when you went into a shop the owner knew your preferences and how far you could stretch your finances.

The Church bells played quite an important part in the activities of the town. The twelve o'clock and eight o'clock curfews were observed and used every day. At twelve midnight on New Year's Eve the bells rang out.

If there was a wedding at the Church and the bells were rung about half an hour before the arrival of the guests, you knew it was going to be well worth watching, as only well off people paid a fee to have the full carillon. People locked their doors and made their way up the brow to the Church.

It was always a pleasant crowd who gathered and it certainly pleased the bride and groom. More often than not, men would have tied a rope across the Church gates and demanded a token to let the bride and groom through. This was all done and accepted with pleasure by the guests and spectators.

Apart from the bells ringing morning and night for Church services, a single bell tolled at eight

The church bell ringers performed an important part of the town's activities

o'clock each Sunday morning for people taking the sacrament. On Shrove Tuesday the bell rang at eleven o'clock instead of twelve. This was a very old custom which gave boys who were apprenticed a half day holiday starting at eleven o'clock. I believe this was the only time they had free to enjoy themselves.

When anyone in the town died, a single bell was tolled for about ten minutes. For a man it was tolled seven times then a lull then repeated again several times. It rang five tolls for a woman and four for a child. A bell tolled all the time at a funeral.

I for one will never forget with what relief and happiness but also great sorrow, we listened to the Church bells which had been silent all those years ringing out loud and clear all day and long into the night, the day that peace was declared. People were laughing and crying in disbelief that the war was over. It was one of the most emotional times I have ever known.

If you were left a widow you were expected to wear black clothing for a year, then you went into what was called half mourning when your clothes would be mauve colour. If you did not follow this procedure you were considered uncaring and flighty. Men wore black ties and a black armband on their coats.

For generations, the Hibbert family rang the curfew bell. I remember Mr. Billy Hibbert who had a shop on the street near the Market Place, closing for a time every day whilst he went to the belfry to ring the twelve o'clock curfew bell. Either he or some member of his family were there to ring the curfew bell at eight o'clock each night. I don't think they were ever a second off time.

The view of Chapel from Park Road, where the fields come right up to the streets.

CHAPTER ~4~

THE WARMING STONE

On the first day of our summer holiday my mother bought Winnie and I a pair of canvas shoes called daps. They had black and white speckled tops and black rubber soles and trimmings. They were meant to save wear and tear of our better shoes as we played in the fields and on the rough road. To us they were heavenly! So light and springy. As soon as we put them on we were skipping along to the Warming Stone on Park Road where we knew our friends would have gathered.

The Warming Stone, part of a brick built boiler house of the brewery, was a thick stone slab about three yards long and two feet in width which lay on top of the boiler house to form its roof. At the front the boiler house had an iron door which opened up the fire hole. This was used to scrape out the embers of the furness that heated the boiler where the beer was brewing.

At the end of the brewing session, the stone slab was warm enough for us to sit on, sheltered from the cold with our knees tucked under our chins, huddled together all snug and comfortable. On Winter evenings if the weather was suitable, after our tea, we used to meet our friends there playing word games, but more often than not telling ghost stories for an hour or so until our parents came for us at bedtime.

The entry to Park Road was an ideal place for us to play all through the year. There was plenty of space for a game of rounders or bowling along with our large wooden hoops. We always had a ball to play with, throwing and catching against the wide chimney of the brewery boiler house. My father was keen on sport and we never asked in vain for money for a ball. They were a bit bigger than a tennis ball but double skin rubber, They were considered a luxury as they cost seven and a ha'pence each.

The big gates of the brewery yard were always open and the paved yard and the beautiful old buildings with the sun filtering through a pleasant background for our games. Across the road was the high wall of Mr. Walker's garden with beautiful trees hanging over it. The extension to the Institute has since been built there. I am glad I can remember it as it used to be.

Mr. Simpson, who owned the brewery, was a kind man and although he was a bachelor he understood children and liked seeing them playing around the brewery. In the Autumn he would come to the yard gates, tease us for a while, then from his pockets take lovely ripe pears, gathered from the tree at the back of the house. We were each given one to eat and

some to take home to our mothers. He would not give any to the older boys. He said they helped themselves to enough over the garden wall.

The older boys played their own games on Park Road. Marbles and other games, but mostly it was a game which involved deftly manoeuvering iron hoops around each other. These hoops were made by relatives and friends at the Matthew Longson's foundry at Town End. I never saw any for sale in the shop. They were controlled by a short length of iron with a loop at one end to hang it up by and a hook at the other end to guide the hoop along.

During the summer holidays most of our time was spent by the stream in Park Fields. On our way we could not resist calling in at Longson's Farm. There was always something to attract us. Being greeted by their lovely collie dog Lassie was one of them. She was so gentle and playful. We all loved her.

Everywhere was always so quiet and peaceful. Just the sounds of the soft clucking of hens in the yard foraging for corn that had been dropped whilst feeding the cows. The sound of milk squirting into a bucket as Tom Longson sat with his cap on back to front milking a cow. The rattle of chains against the side of the byres as the cows contentedly munched their feed of corn and chopped hay. Sometimes we were allowed to carry a box of fodder down the narrow alleyway in front of the byres. It was quite frightening being so close to the cows horns as we put the feed in front of them but it was also an adventure for us.

Down in the meadow corncrakes could be heard croaking and squawking as they fed their young. The meadow grass was almost ready for cutting and the weather signs were being observed to be ready to start at the first signs of a period of dry weather. Then it was all hands to the mowing machine which was all ready and waiting with newly sharpened blades. Beside it was the horse drawn rake and a newly sharpened scythe which was used for cutting parts where the horse and mower could not reach.

Tearing ourselves away from the farm we were on our way, over the road, past the old cottages and the tall horsechestnut trees that would give us so much pleasure in the Autumn gathering conkers from them to play one of our favourite games, conker bashing.

Beyond the cottages there was an iron gate across the road to stop the cattle from straying. At one side was a kissing gate for pedestrians. The gates were very attractive wrought iron with tall heavy stone gateposts to fasten them to.

In the early evening at milking time, the cows would have come up the field and be waiting behind the iron gate, mooing softly and swishing their tails to keep the flies off. Tom would open the gate for them and they would make their way slowly to their stall in the shippon. They all knew their place and never made a mistake.

I remember one day going over to the Warming Stone when for once my friends were not there. I had my hoop with me so I continued over the road and through the gate. The cows were sitting on a mound in the field chewing their cud. I bowled my hoop down the sloping field then up to the cows. For a time I steered my hoop around each one. They were so contented they never moved. I suddenly had a bright idea! I gathered a lot of daisies and made a daisy chain for several cows, then hung them over their horns. I believe there was lots of laughter from Tom when the cows went in at milking time.

There were four quite large houses in Park Road. I remember Mr. and Mrs. Stables and the Partington family who were charming people and very popular in the town. Mr. Partington was a solicitor in Chapel. Across the road to these houses was a flight of steep wooden steps straddling the wall. These led to a small tennis club with two grass courts. This was very exclusive and certainly rare in the district. As the road wound on it was flanked on one side by tall ash trees and a hawthorn hedge. When the hawthorn was in flower the scent from it was almost unbearably strong and in the soft summer breeze you could smell it on the main street.

More often than not when playing in the fields in the summer we took a bunch of flowers home for our mothers. She was always pleased but would never let us take hawthorn blossom into the house. It was supposed to bring bad luck so it was put in a jam jar of water and left outside on the kitchen window sill.

The road sloped down to the stream and over the simple yet beautiful bridge which must have been there for centuries for an access to the ancient Eaves Hall. The top stones of the bridge were wide and chiseled to a point along the centre. What pride those stonemasons must have had in their work to use their craft on a small bridge that was way out in the country and seen by few people.

At the side of the bridge was a large alder tree where blue tits made a nest every year. We watched eagerly for the repetition of a treat we had one year as the parents brought their young one by one out of the nest and stood them side by side along the branch of the tree. The little fluffy yellow chicks were fed, then in turn persuaded to take flight. We were lucky to have been there at the time and I have never forgotten it.

Over the bridge the road curved to two white gates, each one leading up to a drive, one to "Lower Eaves", a beautiful old house owned by Mr. & Mrs. Kerr. The other drive had a lodge inside the gate. This drive led to "Upper Eaves" which was a gentleman's residence and farm. Mr. and Mrs. Samuel Needham lived there.

Mr. and Mrs. Kerr were delightful people. They always gave a penny to us when we opened the gates for their pony and trap to pass through. Mr. Needham could not bear to see us playing on Park Road and pushed us on one side with his walking stick. He was a grumpy looking man and always seemed to have a drip on the end of his nose. His poor little wife was shabbily dressed and very plain, with her hair scraped up into a knot on the top of her head. She walked about half a yard behind her husband and never looked happy. Mr. Needham died first. She lived on at the farm. A few years later she went into the hairdresser's shop and asked them to put a bit of frizz in her hair. It was so sad to think that for all her life she must have been longing to be free like other women she knew.

When we were playing over the Park Fields, we usually went through the Kissing Gate then down the field alongside the low stone wall of the meadow to where the stream had been blocked to make a dam to serve the wadding mill and Sammy Lee's farm. At this point a wooden fence stretched across the water. We were warned never to climb over it as the water was so deep we would drown if we fell in. We were often tempted to cross it as the best flowers seemed to grow on the other side, such as meadow-sweet, forget-me-nots, marsh marigolds, moonpennies and, on the shallow edge, masses of monkey musk.

The stream narrowed as it reached the dam and was deep and very clear. We loved this as strange little fish could be seen darting about. They had slim bodies and large heads with bulging eyes, very like a toad's head. We called them 'bullheads'. It may not have been their real name but it suited them very well.

At this point it was difficult to walk along the bank as the cows came down to drink where the bank was shallow. In wet weather the ground was soft and the cattle made deep imprints with their hooves. In dry weather these were hardened and became rough and uneven to walk on. Supported by stone walling, the brook became fast and deep again and was crossed by a narrow wooden bridge which led into Parmainus Long's fields.

All along the stream, the banks were covered with wild flowers and at times the scent of them was almost overwhelming. We hardly ever crossed the little white bridge as we were so afraid of Parmainus Long. He was elderly with a longish beard and hair, very religious and narrow-minded. I think he considered it a sin if children crossed over the bridge onto his land. If he saw us over on his fields he chased us with a long whip waving in his hand.

After the bridge, large willow trees hung over the stream, their supple branches were ideal for hanging by to swing to and fro across the water. We took our shoes and socks off for this game in case our feet dangled in the water. We were ready for our next pleasure which was

Haymaking was a rollicking time. The grass lay in long shining swathes and there were lots of willing helpers. This is a scene on the Barlow farm.

paddling in the shallower water. We slipped into the water gently and quietly, then stood patiently waiting for the trout to come swimming around our feet or gently lifting large stones in the hope of finding one resting there. They were so beautiful and gentle but moved like lightening if disturbed. Although there were plenty in the stream, I cannot recall seeing anyone fishing for them.

As the brook flowed towards us from the old stone bridge, it was joined by a stream from the Target Field. This was another favourite spot of ours as it was always alive with little jacksharps darting about. We loved the little silver fish and I must admit that we occasionally caught a few in a jam jar to enjoy at home. On reaching the bridge, we sat on the warm stone copings to dry our feet and put our socks and shoes on again .

In Spring and Summer these fields and the stream were a paradise. We did not need toys to play with. We found all the pleasure we needed in nature and we ourselves were part of it. Over the bridge the banks were clay and when the water went low in the Summer we collected tins full of it, which we took to a bank in the field. There were two dead ash trees on it and their roots were exposed, leaving hollows like small caves among them.

We sat on the bank for hours modelling the clay into all manner of shapes and human figures. Above all we made plates, cups and saucers, dishes, that we needed when we played house. We put them under the tree roots and left them to dry, fetching them as we needed them.

One day I went to collect some things and I was staggered to find a beautiful little garden leading up to my tree root. There were little paths with flowers and tiny trees all beautifully arranged. I was a bit frightened as I thought there really must be fairies. Then I heard children's voices calling and a little girl and boy came towards me. They were Kathleen and David Lyal, the children of the new tenants of the house in the field. They had found our clay pots and been most impressed and decided to make a little garden leading to them. We made friends there and then and remained very close for most of our lives.

Playing over in Park Fields was another time that the ancient custom of the ringing of the curfew was used. If we were over there in the mornings, we were told to go home for our dinner when the twelve o'clock curfew sounded and in the evenings to go home for bedtime when we heard the eight o'clock bell.

We were always excited when we went over to Longson's farm and could hear the sound of the mowing machine cutting the grass in the meadow. We knew that haymaking time was here and we were in for a rollicking time in the next few days. The grass lay in long shining swathes and next day the Longson family with lots of willing helpers would be at work tossing and spreading it with pitch forks.

This was very hard work but was carried out until the grass was dry and turned to hay. As this procedure was considered dangerous we were not allowed to help but when with rakes the hay was brought into line again, we did a good job carrying stray bundles to where the hay cocks were being piled, ready to be loaded onto the carts. The horses, Bess or Charlie pulled the heavy loads, almost lost to sight by the overhanging hay. They were backed into the barn to be unloaded. Those horses, sweating as they were, seemed to know that the hay was for their benefit and never gave trouble however tired they must have been.

We children had a picnic in the hayfield and as a special treat drinking pop out of a glass bottle that was secured at the narrow neck by a glass ball which had to be pressed into the wider part of the neck before the pop could run out. By evening we were tired out from helping or simply romping about in the sweet smelling hay and were ready for home. When we arrived, our mother would undress us, and give us a wash down to get rid of the prickly grass seeds sticking to our sweaty skin.

One day during our Summer holidays, I went over to the farm to see if they had started mowing the meadow. As haymaking was a pleasure we always looked forward to it. There was no-one there until I was joined by a boy I knew, called Alfie Livesley. He was the son of the chemist, who had a shop next to the Town Hall. We went through the yard gate into the meadow, then walked along the border of the tall grass until we were stopped by the manure heap which, after being thrown through the muckhole in the shippen, had spread itself well into the meadow.

The heap was deeper than usual as none had been used whilst the meadow was growing. The weather had been very hot and the sun had dried the surface of the heap, leaving a hard crust on it. Alfie was a mischievous boy, and I should have been warned when he ran a few steps up the shallow end of the crusty surface. "Bet you daren't do that", he taunted.

Not to be outdone, I followed suit. This challenge continue for several efforts each one going higher up the heap. "Let's see how far you can go by yourself." Not wanting to be thought a coward, I ran a couple of yards higher. Then the hard crust wore thin, broke under my weight, and I found myself sinking deeper and deeper into the soft manure.

The more I struggled the deeper I went. I was soon waist deep and my shoes had come off. I began to scream with fright and horror. As I went over on my side I floundered about trying to keep my arms free and my head above the surface. The stench was unbearable and made me heave, which did not help. To make matters worse, Alfie disappeared and I was left alone to die, as I thought.

As I became hysterical, my screaming increased and I could not believe it when Sam Longson's face appeared at the muckhole. I was most fortunate that he had come to the farm at that moment, and heard my screams. He could not reach me with his hands, so he found a piece of rope which he flung to me and I managed to catch. Then he pulled with all his might and got me through the muckhole into the shippen. Poor Sam did not know what to do for me as I stood there screaming. Even my hair was plastered with the muck. He got an armful of hay from the barn and tried to wipe some of it off me. It was hopeless as I flung

Possibly the last hayload to go through the streets of Chapel. The picture of Tom Longson and his nephew Colin, gives a good idea of the size of the heavy loads which used to overhang horse and cart!

myself about. Someone appeared at the shippen door and Sam said, "Fetch her father."

Now all the neighbours knew that "Ada's fallen in the muck heap", and they stood at their doors waiting for my father to bring me home. I think he was shocked when he saw me and realised that I could not possibly walk home. So, picking me up, muck as well, he had to carry me home. It was impossible to take me into the house in such a state so my mother rolled out the dolly tub and filled it with warm water, stripped off my filthy clothes, then lifted me naked into the tub. By this time there was quite an audience of neighbours watching my plight.

I often think how fortunate I was that Sam happened to come to the farm in time to save me from what I am certain would have been a horrible end to a young life…

Sam Longson…he really did save my life that summer's day.

CHAPTER

~ 5 ~

WHERE HAVE ALL THE TREES GONE?

Chapel was built more or less in a straight line from Barmoor Clough to Tunstead Milton. It was divided into four areas - Town End, Market Street, High Street and Crossings, which continued over the level towards Whaley Bridge. From Town End to the railway bridge was the commercial part. Almost all the shops were there. Crossings had a couple of shops but was mostly residential. Chapel was encircled by the very large houses built by wealthy businessmen from Manchester, who were mostly in the cotton trade.

For a time these people seemed alien to Chapel, with their nannies, servants, gardeners and grooms, but they found employment for people and eventually most of them integrated with the townsfolk and became a great asset, joining in at most local events, especially sport. They built a golf course, which is still one of Chapel's greatest attractions.

There were three churches in the town,Wesleyan Chapel in Town End, Primitive Methodist on Market Street and the Parish Church in the Market Place. The Wesleyans and the Church had their own schools. Teaching standards were high at both schools and I think this came from keen competition between them. Regrettably when I was a child there was animosity between the two churches. We considered the children from over the brook in Town End as our 'enemies' and vice versa. There were times when we stood either side of the brook shouting insults at each other. I can never remember being rebuked by our parents for doing this. It was never denied that there was childish jealousy amongst the adults as well.

Fortunately, as we got older, the idiocy stopped. I think the Great War had a lot to do with it. Whatever your religion we all stood side by side and were united to serve together as best we could. So many of my friends are Wesleyan and when we discuss this situation we cannot believe that it could possibly have been like that, but all agree that it was so.

Coming to the end of a long line of chestnut trees, which once highlighted the entrance to the town on either side of the road. People often walked along here just to admire their beauty. Where have they gone?

Despite the fact that there were several mills in the town, Chapel remained rural. The fields came right up to the street and there were gates where the cows used to muster at milking time every day in the summer. It was a pleasant sight to see them walking slowly, unharrassed by traffic down to the farm leaving as they passed a sweet country farm smell.

The building line was softened in places by groups of trees, many of them overhanging the road. Starting near the New Inn there was a lovely Georgian house with a large garden where Mr. & Mrs. George Pink lived. It was called Chestnut House. Large chestnut trees grew there and shaded the road. Across from it was another large house where a doctor used to live. Later it became the childrens' home. There were lots of horse chestnut trees there as well and coming under the railway bridge I used to think that these trees made a lovely entrance to the town centre, especially in the Autumn.

After this came the Vicarage and opposite from it was the old parsonage. Both had large gardens which came right to the narrow pavement. It was a treat in the Spring to see the colours as trees flowering in the both gardens met over the street. The colours of red hawthorn, lilac and laburnum was a beautiful sight and people used to take a walk up the street just to enjoy the picture it made and to smell the perfume from the blossom.

In the croft next to the brewery cottages a row of lime trees hung over the wall and shaded the street and again at Cooper's coalyard across the road (where the big service station is now located), lime trees softened the line of the stone buildings.

There were also lots of trees in Town End, especially in Miss Anderson's garden where fruit trees in blossom were always a picture as was the massive pear tree that grew up the front of the house. There were large trees in the manse gardens and around the school. In the spring, summer and autumn, people walked the street for the pleasure of seeing the beautiful picture made by the trees. Where have so many of them gone?

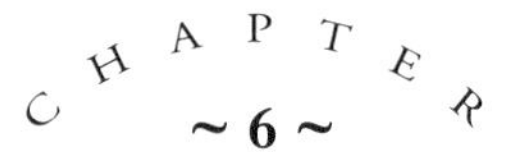

LOCAL CHARACTERS

With the exception of shops, most places of work finished for the week at twelve noon on Saturdays when wages were paid out. Saturday afternoon was a busy time for the shops as husbands and wives usually went out together to spend as much as they could on food and things necessary for the home and family. Shops were well stocked and there were plenty of them to serve the town. There were no mixed businesses and each shop sold only goods particular to its trade. There were no ready packed goods at the grocers. Everything was delivered in bulk and weighed and packaged when it was bought.

Until the 1920s everything came into the town by train and was delivered to the shops from the station by horse and dray. One determined young local character was ***Sam Longson***, the farmer's boy who saved my life when I fell into the muck heap. He was the third son of the farmer Samuel Longson, and he was developing a local haulage business with the horse and dray his father used for delivering milk and for carting gunpowder to the quarries. Sam used to pick up the mail at the station every morning at five o'clock. Products from the farms, such as milk, went by train into Manchester.

During the national rail strike in the 1920s, churns of milk from the dairy farms around Chapel were just left at the station to go sour. Striking railwaymen refused to take them into Manchester. Young Sam decided to do something about them. By 1920 he had a Model T Ford wagon and, with improving roads, believed it was possible to deliver milk from the farms around Chapel into their customers in Manchester. He went around the farms picking up the milk churns and taking them directly into the city. This was how he became a pioneer in distance haulage by road.

Farmers soon saw the benefit of having their milk picked up by Sam, rather than having to

Before the Storm: The Rev. E. Standfast's Young Men's Class at Town End Methodist Church in 1911-1914 before a number of them volunteered for service in the First World War 1914-18. From left, back row: F. Cottrill, E. Sidebotham, A. Marchington, S. Ibbotson, P. Pinder, J. Marchington, T. Kirk, B. Sidebotham, N. Longson. Sitting middle row: Tom Longson, H. Carrington, Rev. Standfast, J. Muir, J. Ibbotson. Front row: Matthew Longson, A. Turner, Frank Longson, Wilfred Needham.

deliver their churns to Chapel station every morning. Sam also realised that he could help local traders by filling his empty wagon with all sorts of goods for the return journey to Chapel. By the 1960s he had more than 100 eight-wheeler wagons and one of the biggest haulage businesses in the North of England, mainly transporting limestone from the quarries to the industrial areas of Britain. When he retired, William Hickey, the columnist in *The Daily Express,* called Sam the 'man who moved mountains'. In the 1960s and 70s he was famous as Chairman and President of Derby County Football Club, the English League champions, and was awarded the OBE at Buckingham Palace. The farmer's boy from Chapel had gone a long way. The business still flourishes at Town End garage.

In the early part of the Century, tea came to Chapel in large thin wooden boxes lined with silver paper. Butter was in lightweight barrels. This was put on a ceramic dish when opened and the butter was then cut through in even slices about three inches thick by a wire with-two wooden handles. Cheeses came in bulk as well, sealed with layers of muslin cloth. There was little variety of cheese. It was mostly Cheshire or Cheddar.

Dried fruit and sugar were sold from their containers and packed very neatly as you bought them in thick bags usually coloured pink or blue. Sugar was always put in the blue bag. They were very deftly folded and tied with a thin twine from a ball which was in a small container fastened onto the edge of the counter.

The larger shops had bacon slicers which were turned by a handle. These shops also had mahogany topped counters and shelves on the wall behind it with small drawers along it in which were kept nutmegs, ginger and all kinds of spices. Biscuits were sold from large square tins. The lid was removed and replaced with one with a glass top so that you could choose without opening the lid too often. They were put on a display frame in front of the counter.

Many of the shops were privately owned and many of these people were real characters which I would enjoy recalling. They all added to the colour of everyday life in Chapel.

Winter milk 'carriages' awaiting the train to Manchester at Chapel Central Station

At the bottom of the broad steps which lead up to the Market Place is a stone built house called The Hollies. ***John Sidebotham*** (right) lived there with his sister and her husband. He was a remarkable man, possibly the best-known and respected in Chapel. He was short and plump with a heavy face and a large nose on which he wore gold-rimmed eye glasses. He had a shop, across the road from his house, where he sold jewellery, antique furniture, china and glassware, all high class and beautiful. His nephew Tom worked for him repairing clocks and watches.

At every concert in the village John was asked to take the chair, introducing in turn all the performers. More often than not John was the best turn of the evening. As he stood up to announce the first item on the programme there would be a movement in the audience and a smile would pass over every face in anticipation of a story he was about to tell, full of humour and dry wit. He usually started in a rather slow, dreamy voice, "I remember a gentleman once saying to me…" then would follow a witty story of bygone days.

He was invited to all the "do's" in Chapel be it a banquet, private dinner party or opening a sale of work. He was very popular and a great asset to the town. Every morning at precisely nine o'clock old John would emerge from his house carrying a saucer of milk for his cat at the shop. He opened the heavy iron studded door to the shop, entered, then emerged a few minutes later to remove the wooden shutters from the shop windows.

Few people passed the shop without stopping to enjoy the lovely things displayed there. Silver, antiques, lots of Georgian silver, ivory framed miniatures, and a wonderful display of jewellery, including wristlet watches. He seemed to specialise in cut glass bowls and vases.

Everyone went to John's shop for engagement rings, wedding rings, Christening mugs, etc.

On entering the shop you were, for a few moments, aware only of the dim light and the quietness after the street sounds outside. Only the tick tock of the grandfather clock standing against the wall could be heard. Then through the gloom you realise that old John is sitting by the fire reading *The Manchester Guardian*. He becomes aware of you, puts down the paper and changes his eye glasses as he moves towards the glass topped counter.

He looks hard at you for a moment, then with a smile of recognition smiles at you and says "Oh! It's you Ada, I did not recognise you for a minute. Isn't it a lovely day?" You agree then tell him that you want to buy a wedding present. He then says, in his slow singing voice "Now I know it's no use showing you anything cheap Ada, you have such good taste" A very astute business man is old John knowing that a bit of flattery is an excuse for putting his most expensive things on the counter.

He now proceeds to put some sheets of white tissue paper on the counter. Then without hurry opens the glass doors to the window display. He brings out a large glass bowl and puts it reverently on the counter. "Now isn't that a beauty" he says. "Real hand cut glass".

He then brings out some choice bits of silver and other luxurious items. You ask the price of the bowl. He says "Now that is real hand cut glass, just feel the weight of it". You ask the price of it. "Five pounds, but being that it is you Ada four pounds ten". There is a longish pause whilst you make up your mind. "I'm thinking I shall have to close the shop, trade is so bad. How's your father Ada? I haven't seen him for a long time". So the conversation goes on.

He knows exactly how to keep your mind off the price and in the quiet peace of the shop your mind is dimmed to the reality of the cost so you choose the cut glass bowl which is more than you intended to pay. "Oh, she will love it Ada. You have such good taste". Really I hate cut glass!

Robert Fergusson was a personality worth mentioning. He was a tall, elegant man with a

In the heart of the main street, this beautiful cottage once belonged to a Miss Goddard. It stood opposite the Royal Oak Inn, at the junction with Rowton Road.

large waxed moustache. In the summertime he almost looked dapper wearing a straw cadie hat. He had two shops on Market Street. One next to Sidebotham's and the other lower down the hill. The top shop was a men's outfitters where he sold all manner of clothing from shoes, jackets and trousers suitable for workmen to boys and men's tailored suits which he made on the premises.

A few shops lower down the street was a ladies shop. A real gem as under the sharp eye of his manager, ***Miss Nellie Simpson***, everything one needed for home dress making was in stock. Pins, needles, elastic, tape, corset laces, you could not ask for the wrong thing.

Miss Simpson was tall and thin. She still dressed in the Victorian style and always in black. The shop was low and dark, crammed from ceiling to floor with shelves and things hanging on hooks from the ceiling. It was like entering a cave. It was very small and at one end was an opening into another room. You could not see inside this other room but there was always a gleam from a fire reflected through the opening.

One day my mother sent me to the shop for some buttons. For once in a way Nellie was not in the shop and my curiosity made me explore into the firelit room. Sitting by the fireside in a large armchair was a very old lady wearing a white lace cap. She looked to me in the subdued firelight like a witch and when she asked me "Who's little body are you" I was convinced that she was a witch and was after my body. I turned and ran all the way home. It was a long time before I was convinced that the witch was Mr. Fergusson's mother.

There was no transport so Miss Simpson had to walk to and from work every day. As shops did not close until eight o'clock at night she must have been tired out before setting out for home. It was a long way to walk to and from New Smithy, especially in winter time.

Ben Eaton was a cobbler. He had a shop on the main street near the bottom of Church Brow. It was a very popular meeting place for local men to discuss the weekend football matches, as Ben was a great football enthusiast. He was a plain looking man with a large nose and a red face. He wore steel rimmed glasses which did not enhance his appearance. Even so, his face was as pleasant as his character.

The back of his shop was dark and gloomy and rather frightening to us children. There were leather hides hanging in the dimness at the back, looking ghostly in the dim light. Also there was a large shop window where Ben had his work bench. Nothing passed up or down the street that Ben did not notice. The street was his stage and all the actors known to him.

We used to gather at his window to marvel at his skill of taking some tacks in his hand and transferring them to his mouth, holding them between his teeth, he would take up his hammer, start whistling a hymn tune, then he would take a tack out of his mouth and hammer it into the shoe in rhythm to the hymn tune. It was fascinating to watch and I never heard that he swallowed any, but it was always expected that one day we would hear the sad news. In the quiet of Chapel main street, often the only sound was of Ben's whistling as he hammered and saved yet another sole!

Next to Ben Eaton's shop was a barber called ***Teddie Meyer***. He also was short in stature and rotund. He was always rather flashily dressed and had a large moustache twirled and waxed at each end, stretching across his face like two handlebars. Most of his trade was cutting hair as most men shaved themselves, using a long bladed razor which folded into a handle for safety. Safety razors as we know them had not been invented in those days. Mr. & Mrs. Meyer were pleasant people and popular in town.

After this came the telephone exchange. It was a part of the house where Mrs. Kirk and her daughter lived and they were in charge of it. There were very few private phones. I remember that the Dog Inn was No.3. You could use the telephone in the Exchange but you were very careful whom you called and what you said as all was heard by the Kirk family and you could have no secrets.

At the top of the street next to the Dog Inn and grocers shop was ***Frank Bramwell's*** saddlers work place or shop as it was called. In no way could I call Mr. Bramwell a character. He was a tall, quiet and dignified man. He must have had a good business as he was the only saddler in the town. It was a long narrow low ceilinged room with a small window at the end. Hanging on the walls were horse collars and bridles with saddles and reins hanging over the narrow counter. Mr. Bramwell would be sitting on a high stool wearing a leather apron stitching away on some piece of saddlery, usually by hand. He wore a kind of mitten which had a thick pad of leather in the centre of his hand with which he used to push the large needle threaded with catgut through the worn or broken leather. I was attracted to that workshop with its white-washed walls and horse and leather smell.

Between Fergusson's two shops, ***Mrs. Boswell*** had a cafe., She was a plump lady, very nice to look at and she must have been getting on a bit as she had curly white hair. I suppose it was a cafe, but in a rough and tumble way. It was another long low-ceilinged room with two trestle tables going the length of it. These were covered with white tablecloths and the seats were long narrow benches. Mrs. Boswell was noted for her home-boiled ham which was delicious and very popular in the town.

It was always a busy day for her on market day as farmers queued to get a seat for a ham sandwich. On these days, Mrs. Boswell was always hot and bothered but she was usually helped out by her husband, who was a little man, as round as an alarm clock. He worked as a plate layer on the railway.

Lower down the street ***Mrs. Appleton*** with two of her daughters also had a cake shop and cafe. This was a much more refined establishment and their cakes, bread and pies were enjoyed by everybody, especially their parkin, the like of which has never been made since. I remember that they had the first biscuit we saw after all the years of the First World War. They were custard creams.

They baked bread and cakes and these were delivered by Mr. Appleton in a horse drawn vehicle which was like a small caravan with a white canvas covering. It was a strange looking set up especially when Mr. Appleton was walking, as he was a small man with a heavy black moustache and he had a wooden leg.

Next to Fergussons was ***Raymond Beard's*** hardware shop. He sold every household necessity, from tin openers to tableware to carpets, all manner of tools and paraffin. He had four brothers living with him, also a sister and her husband. Only one brother, called Jacob, and the brother-in-law went out to work. One of them was never seen as he broke his leg when working for his father. He took to his bed and never got up again (so it was said). The other two were identical twins who seemed to have a very easy life being kept by the others.

Raymond was a small man with very wrinkled skin, tinged yellow from all the cigarettes he smoked. There always seemed to be a "dimp" in the corner of his mouth. Every day he was dressed in shabby black trousers, waistcoat and a grubby shirt without a collar. He always wore an old bowler hat when serving in the shop.

It was almost impossible to tell the twins apart. The same height and width and each with a large drooping moustache. Their attire was always the same. Black suits decorated with a large heavy watch chain across their fronts, black leggings up to their knees and each wearing a large black trilby hat which along with their heavy black moustaches made them look more Mexican than English. They carried short walking sticks which made them stoop to the same level.

Every night whatever the weather, they'd set out for a long walk, carrying a lighted lantern. If you were out to some function or other until the early hours of the morning, you would be almost certain to meet Jim and Joe wending their way home.

As I have said, we children did not venture over the stream to Town End. Even so, I liked going with my mother. The shops were good and I always thought it looked much more refined than Market Street. Immediately over the bridge was the Co-op. A large shop where they only sold groceries. For all purchases a token was given which gave a dividend on the amount spent. This was redeemed on a certain date which people called "Divi" day. The shop was always busy on that day as the value of "divi" was an asset to wages coming in.

Next to the Co-op was a butcher's shop owned by Mitchells who also had a small-holding on Burrfields. Across the road was a very nice stone house where the Ibbotsons lived. They owned the engineering mill that was set well back from the road. It was a one-storey building built of brick and had a tallish chimney stack. The space between the works and road they kept as a flower garden. With the red brick mill and the flowers, it was a good subject for a painting.

There was another attractive house next to the Ibbotsons where there lived a very refined lady called Miss Hyde. Her servant, who had devoted her life to serve her, lived with her.

After this, there were two more shops and a house where the Oxleys lived. Then there was a wide open space with a road leading to Sammy Lee's farm and a large house which was the Children's Home. The Children's Home was for children who had lost their parents and were homeless. They were not local children. Some of them came from as far away as Sheffield.

They were well cared for and soon settled into their new life and integrated with other children and became part of the young life in Chapel. More often than not they were families and when they became adult found work in the district and eventually met and married a local boy or girl. In later years the Home was moved to a larger house on High Street, called Cromwell House, which is now the Social Services Offices.

In the Spring, the trees in the garden of the Methodist Manse at Town End, laburnum and pink hawthorn, were a colourful display. Across the road was Carrington's Shop where they sold household goods, china, pottery, tools, nails, screws and everything you would need. It was a very popular shop and we often called there with our parents.

Mr Simpson's house (on the right), situated on Market Street, where next to it three unusual red brick cottages stood with a steep flight of steps going up to each door. (Painting by the author).

When I walk up Market Street, I pass what was once a most attractive and interesting group of buildings - The Old Brewery, which was alongside and below the Memorial Institute. Very few people seem to know where the brewery was or that it even existed and when I tell them its location they wonder why I am nostalgic about such a dreary and decrepit place.

However, before the first World War, it was a small but thriving village industry owned by the Simpson family and managed by ***Mr. Sam Simpson***. He lived in a lovely old house facing onto Market Street. The brewery buildings were at the back of it on Park Road.

Next to it there were three most unusual red brick cottages. Each one had an arch covering a steep flight of steps to the front door. The cottages were high because they were built over the cellars. Three families lived here called Lomas, Nichols and Nall. They were all employed by Simpsons.

Over Park Road the brewery entrance had two wide wooden gates opening onto a paved yard and a compact group of lovely old buildings. One was an open fronted shed which sheltered the huge boiler. The outer wall of this was on Park Road and against it was the stoke hole and the tall blue brick factory chimney. The back of the house, with a lovely old door, came into the yard and next to it a building where the cooper worked. After this the stables and cart shed. The saddle room had a wide open entrance and above it up a flight of stone steps was the storeroom. The small staff were local men who worked happily together under the kindly eye of Mr. Sam. There was a quietness and harmony about the whole place and on brewing days this was enhanced by the rich aroma of brewing beer.

Mr. Sam was a great favourite of we children. When the fruit was ripe in his lovely garden he would be waiting for us coming out of school with his pockets full of apples and pears to give to us. He never gave any to the boys. He said they helped themselves enough over the garden wall and those who were too young and too small at the moment would have their day later on!

The last load to leave the brewery. In its later years the brewery was sold by the Simpsons to Stancliffe Brothers, brewers of Macclesfield.

Mr. Simpson was a tall, elegant man with mutton chop whiskers. He always wore a cap. The garden at the brewery was a secret place behind a high wall. Occasionally, Mr. Simpson would allow Winnie and me to go with him as he tended his plants and trees. This was a great treat for us and we really thought it was a magic place.

He would take us across the paved yard to the back door of the house. A large pear tree grew up the wall of this lovely sandstone house. While he fetched the key from the house, his housekeeper would give us a biscuit. Now began the exciting part of our walk to the garden. We went across the cobbled yard, past the saddle room then into the dim light as we passed the stable, then under the cart shed which at the end became almost total darkness.

Mr. Simpson would then fumble with the key in the lock and slowly open the heavy door to reveal, like magic, a scene of dazzling sunlit colour . It was like entering Fairyland after the dark of the cart shed. We slowly walked through the flowers, through the rockery with its strange formations of limestone rocks found I suppose in the Dove Holes quarries. Then to the orchard with its lines of well trimmed fruit trees.

By this time, we were becoming impatient to get to our greatest treat. This was a large greenhouse built against a wall. Eventually he started up the red brick path towards it. He unlocked the door and we followed him in, as quiet as mice, we were so awed. Along the wall was a flowering tree cut to perfection to fit the wall. Benches came down in tiers and were full of the most colourful plants in pots and there were hanging baskets with brilliantly coloured flowers and dainty ferns trailing down. We were warned not to touch the primulas as they could give us eczema.

Then we were taken to the rockery end. This was a separate house leading from the flowers to almost total green. There was a rock garden built from high up the wall containing most wonderfully, a trickling stream which passed between the stones into a deep stone well let into the floor. There were water plants growing in it. We stood very quietly waiting for

The big gates of the Brewery were always open. There was a quietness and harmony about the whole place and on brewing days this was enhanced by the rich aroma of brewing beer.

the large trout that lived there to put in an appearance. Eventually he came - slow, heavy and rather dull-looking. I think this must have been due to his age. Mr. Simpson told us that the trout was 13 years old. Whether this was true or not it all added to the glamour of our visit.

At the end of the visit, we were given a bunch of flowers to take home to our mother. To this day, whenever I smell the delicious odour of a greenhouse my mind goes back to the big fat trout and Mr. Simpson's magical garden.

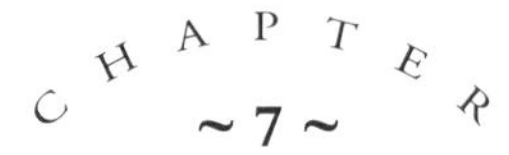

THE WORKING WEEK

For mothers and wives the weekdays passed with routine monotony, each day allocated a certain chore. I will write at some length about Mondays as without detail I could not make you believe the drudgery of wash days...

It was different waking up on Monday mornings. There was an atmosphere in the house. Different sounds and smells. The smell of scorched paper and burning wood coming up from the kitchen. My mother walking across the landing sounded hurried and purposeful. The bedroom door being flung open and my sister and I jostled out of bed. Pillowcases stripped off and sheets removed unceremoniously and dropped in piles on the floor. Our dirty stockings and underclothes gathered up and taken downstairs along with sheets and pillowcases.

Downstairs in the kitchen, the fire crackled, burning steadily under the wash boiler in the corner. The boiler was already full of water heating up to fill the dolly tub. My father, with some impatience, pulled the heavy iron mangle into the middle of the floor. My mother cutting slices off the remainder of the Sunday joint made sandwiches for my father to take for his dinner. Cutting a piece of cake, screwing sugar and tea into a little packet for his "brew up" then putting it into a triangular shaped wicker basket, closing the lid with the handle and fastening it down with a metal skewer.

My sister and I eating our breakfast of Quaker Oats and toast as quietly as two little mice. Monday morning was not a day to play up or misbehave. One learned early to avoid the industry in the kitchen on wash-day, especially on wet days or in winter. Washing-day was almost slavery where there was a large family. There were no special facilities in cottages. All had to be done in the kitchen. It needed strength and great persistence to get through a wash-day and the days of drying and ironing that followed. There was the determination not to be outdone by one's neighbours. There was much competition in a village about housekeeping abilities and doing things the "right way". If you took a "short cut" to minimise the task, it was whispered "She's not very particular"! Said with tight lips and a knowing nod of the head.

After my father had left for work and we for school, my mother rolled the dolly tub into the kitchen from the yard. It was made of oak with iron bands round it and was far too heavy to carry. It was placed in front of the mangle. Whilst the water in the boiler heated up, the clothes were sorted. Woollens for washing and rinsing, cottons for boiling and those that needed starching and blueing. A bar of Knights Castile soap was taken out of the cupboard where it had been put to make it "go further" by drying it to a hardness. It was cut into pieces and some grated into dolly tub and boiler.

By this time, after several stokings of the fire under the boiler, the water was hot enough to transfer to the dolly tub. The boiler was in the corner of the kitchen. It was made of cast iron, and was held in place by a sturdy brick structure. It was large enough to dip a bucket into the water and was covered by a wooden lid. Under the boiler was the fire hole with bars in front and an iron door. At the back was a flue to take the draught and smoke away.

Carrying buckets of water from boiler to tub was another strenuous job, plus the fact that you were almost blinded by the steam which rapidly filled the kitchen. This, of course, meant opening the back door, however cold the weather might be.

Next the dolly peg was brought out from the bottom of the pantry. The dolly peg was, I suppose, the forerunner of a washing machine. It had a base like a small round stool with five short legs splayed out from it. A turned piece of wood about 2ft long was fastened to the centre and through the top of this was a wooden bar.

When the clothes in the tub had been well soaped, the dirtiest parts were rubbed hard by hand, which took considerable time and usually at the end of the day, fingers were red and raw.

This was done whilst kneeling on the stone floor in front of the tub. After this the dolly peg was put into the tub of clothes, then grasping each side of the wooden bar it was turned backwards and forwards in a rhythmic movement. It was really hard work as the clothes were heavy to move about in the water and being in a bending position made your back ache.

Later, a new device came onto the market. It was called a rubbing board. It was about 18 inches wide, usually made of steel, but sometimes thick glass. This was ribbed across and when fixed to the side of the tub the clothes were rubbed up and down on the ribbing. This made things much more comfortable and less painful to the hands, but it was still hard work.

Eventually, a soap powder was produced. It came on the market under the name of "Compo". This was distrusted at first, but it certainly removed grime and stains with much less effort and gradually people accepted it and didn't feel guilty about finding an easier way to do the washing.

Now came one of the really hard tasks. The clothes were lifted out of the tub a few at a time and eased through the rollers on the mangle. Turning the heavy wheel by its handle, the clothes were guided through the rollers dropping into a basket placed on the floor at the back of the mangle. Sometimes, the clothes would go through quite easily, then would come a knotted bunch which could not be separated. Then the screw was released at the top of the mangle which adjusted the rollers to the thickness of the clothes going through.

The mangle had to be very sturdy to stay firmly on the floor whilst the clothes were going through. It was made of heavy cast iron, and was really quite a beautiful object, both in its proportions and by the fact that its side and top were moulded into an ornate design. After a time the rollers would rot and leave a gap in the middle. This meant a job for the local joiner who came to the house to replace them from a stock of rollers he kept for emergencies.

The clothes that needed boiling were first rubbed by hand in the dolly tub then transferred

The author's painting in pastel, done many years ago, still brings to life the drudgery of wash day.

to the boiler. Whilst the boiler was getting to boiling point (and this had to be watched, as the boiler boiling over was a disaster, flooding all around it and often putting out the fire and fillingthe kitchen with steam) the next lot of clothes were put into the tub and rubbed and dollied, then turned through the mangle. These were usually the woollens, socks, stockings and jumpers. They all had to be hand rubbed.

When all had been washed in the dolly tub, the water was emptied down the sink and refilled for rinsing. When it came to rinsing the clothes my mother was fortunate that by this time the fire in the living room had burnt up and had heated the water in the back boiler to give her hot water from the tap in the kitchen sink. I think that rinsing must have been done in cold water in cottages where they were not so fortunate.

Now all the rinsed clothes had to be put through the mangle, not once, but many times to get out as much water as possible. Remember that there were no synthetic materials which hold little water. In those days everything was either cotton or wool that held a lot of water however many times you put them through the wringer. This made drying so difficult. Once more the tub was emptied. By this time the clothes in the boiler were ready. Using a wooden bar, the clothes were lifted out into a large enamel bowl. This procedure filled the kitchen with dense steam which penetrated to all parts of the house through ill fitting doors.

White clothes needed starching and blueing, so, the dolly blue was brought into action. This was a small little stick and a piece of cotton cloth with blue powder packed into it and tied at the top with thin string, leaving a small piece of wood for a handle. This was then moved about in the bowl of starch until the exact colour was reached. Over-blueing clothes made them dry a nasty grey colour!

The water which was left in the tub after wringing the whites was then used for dirtier articles such as aprons and my father's overalls. It was then emptied down the sink and the tub was refilled for rinsing the whites. The water was changed twice or more to make absolutely sure that the clothes would be snow white when dried. Finally, they were dipped separately in the starch, then once more put several times through the wringer.

In between all the to-ing and fro-ing from tub to boiler and sink, an eye was kept on the weather and if there was a possibility of a bit of wind and no rain, the clothes already in the basket would be pegged out, however cold it was. By this time clothing and hair would be damp and I'm sure lots of women got pneumonia this way.

On a Summer's day there was pleasure in hanging clothes on the line in the warm sunshine, then propping them up with the wooden clothes prop. Standing for a few minutes to admire the picture of clothes billowing in the light wind against a blue sky. A small reward for all your effort.

By now the children would be home from school for their mid-day meal. There were no school dinners in those days. All had to be halted in the kitchen to make a sandwich and a drink for them and often for the babies and younger children who were already at home.

Going back to the washing was grim, everything had become soggy and cold, but the routine had to go on. Rubbing, rinsing, mangling, until all was finished. Now the tub had to be emptied by dipping a bucket into it and carrying each bucketful to empty down the sink. This was not easy as the sinks were usually shallow stone sided and the water soon slopped over the side.

Next the boiler was emptied in the same way, making steam all the time. When the boiler had been wiped dry, the fire was raked from under the boiler making much dust to mix with the steam. The ashes were carried to the ashpit in the yard. Then the mangle was wiped as dry as possible and trundled back to the wall.

The kitchen floor was stone flagged and the final chore of wash day was scrubbing the floor on hands and knees, then yellow stoning it. When this was dry, the hearth rug was shaken outside and brought into the kitchen.

My mother made these rugs, as most people did, during the Winter from snips of cloth taken from old clothes, cut into small lengths then pegged through a piece of hessian with a special hook. These rugs were often quite beautiful as people were skilful at making patterns of the different coloured cloth, but they were heavy to handle and shake.

On Summer days there was almost a light hearted atmosphere in the house as clothes dried quickly out of doors. As they were brought in they were folded roughly ready for damping down for ironing. However, on wet days and worse still Winter days, the house was filled with gloom. Everything had to be dried indoors. Clothes maidens around the fire steaming

It is difficult to think how different clothing was in those days...
flannelette petticoats for girls and woollen long johns for boys.
Children at Town end c.1912.

away. Clothes put on top of the oven and over the oven door, hanging from fire irons and fender, any place you could find to dry something.

If you were lucky and lived in a house with fairly high ceilings, you could have a clothes rack which held a lot of clothes and pulled up and down from the ceiling, but cottages had very low ceilings and this luxury was not possible.

It is difficult to think how different clothing was in those days. Frills and flounces galore. Flannelette petticoats. Long bloomers down to your knees. Men's pants were woollen long johns. Women's vests were combinations. Flannelette sheets and woollen socks and stockings. All making wash day an unbelievably hard task. There was also a season for washing blankets, but there lies another story!

At bedtime on bad days we were undressed by the fire, wrapped in a shawl and taken up to bed which had been heated with a warming pan. Steam penetrated everywhere. There was a dampness in the atmosphere and a smell of washing. Next morning was a depressing sight downstairs, with damp washing and piles of dry clothes. We were glad to get off to school and my father to work, leaving my mother to sort out the mess.

Tuesday was ironing day. If the weather had been good for drying on washday some of the ironing would get done then, which was a great relief. Ironing was a gruelling task with the hot steam coming from the item of clothing and the heat coming from the fire as you bent to change the iron which was heating there.

All materials were either cotton, silk or wool, all holding a good weight of water. They would have been damped down the night before and were all ready and neatly folded. A frame was hooked onto the bars of grate which held the iron close to the fire, leaving the handles free and easy to hold. The heat was tested by spitting onto the iron. When it was considered to be the right temperature the iron was rubbed with a piece of soap to make it smooth and to remove any ash from it. This was then rubbed off with a piece of cloth and all was ready. As each piece was finished, it was neatly folded and put over a clothes maiden in front of the fire to air. By the time we came home from school, the house would be warm and usually there was a good smell of stew to compensate for the dreary meals of wash day which were usually potatoes fried-up from Sunday dinner and the remnants of the joint.

Wednesday was cleaning upstairs day. This was no easy task as floors were swept with a long brush, rugs and mats taken out into the yard, shaken and brushed by hand. Chamber pots were emptied into a bucket and carried downstairs to the W.C. Of course, this was an everyday chore. Beds were made, flock mattresses turned and pounded, the same with bolsters and pillows, sheets spread on, then two or more blankets covered by a quilt.

Sweeping the stair carpet was another "hands and knees" job, with dustpan and brush. Not easy going down backwards, especially as so many women suffered from rheumatism. All this must be done before the children came home at dinner time.

Wednesday was also bread making day. A cloth was put on the table along with a large scrubbed bread board, a pansion, flour, yeast soaking in warm water and a little salt and fat.

Flour was put into the pansion, the fat and salt rubbed in and the yeast poured over it. After stirring for a time the dough was kneaded with both hands until it became pliable and smooth. It was then turned over to put smooth side on top, covered with a clean tea towel and put on a stool in front of the fire for the yeast to rise the dough. When it was ready, it was taken out and put onto the floured board, kneaded again, then cut into wedges and fitted into bread tins. They were left on top of the oven to rise a bit more then put into the oven to bake.

When we came home from school, especially in Winter, it was lovely coming into a warm kitchen with the delicious smell of new baked bread cooling on the dresser.

Thursday was another busy day which I think my mother enjoyed, despite the fact that it was market day and she would have relatives who were all farmers calling in for a chat and a cup of tea. It was a cake and pastry making day. The fire was stoked up to heat the oven, a

cloth put on the table, and all necessary equipment brought from the bottom on the pantry where it was stored. Flour, fat, sugar and eggs were at the ready. The currants and raisins were washed and more often than not twigs from the fruit bushes had to be removed.

The pies were made first and cooked whilst the cakes were prepared. Cake tins were greased ready for the cake mixture which was well beaten in a large bowl then transferred to the tins. Sponge cakes were a favourite and near Bonfire Night parkin was made and kept to mature.

You can imagine what it was like coming home from school on a cold Winter day into a kitchen filled with the delicious smell of cakes baking in the oven. My mother used to save the mixing bowl for us to scrape out and eat. It was a great treat and we usually finished it off with our fingers, so as not to waste a scrap!

We usually had a light tea on Thursday as there was plenty of seconds to follow. Quite often we had kippers which were hooked onto a wire frame with a handle. This was fastened onto the grate and cooked. They were always delicious when eaten with Wednesday's new baked bread.

Friday was kitchen cleaning day. Hard and dirty work for our mothers. We were always glad to be off to school on that day. After washing up the breakfast dishes, the pantry was cleaned, the heavy pegged rug taken into the yard, shaken and brushed. The fireguard, fender and firearms cleaned and polished. The long enamelled strip that was decorated like tiles was washed and removed. Ashes from the fire, which had not been lighted, were raked out over an iron grid under which was a deep hole. The ashes and small cinders were raked into the hole and any too big for the grid were put back into the fireplace making a foundation for lighting the fire. After about three weeks the pit was full. It was very heavy work scooping it out by the bucketful and emptying it into the ash pit in the yard. The bars of the grate were black-leaded and the decorative parts cleaned with a piece of emery paper. The hearth was scrubbed and the fender put back in place. The stone flagged floor was scrubbed then the hearth rug put back in place. The fire was lighted and all was finished except for the cleaning of the windows.

You were certainly rewarded for all the hard work by the appearance of a shining kitchen. After tea on Fridays, at every cottage, husbands and wives would be outside their house with brooms and a bucket of water, windows were cleaned, step and window sills scrubbed and yellow stoned. The flags and the gutter were swilled and cleaned with the broom.

Chapel Main Street was always spick and span and the people were proud to have it so.

My sister and I looked forward to Friday night. It was bath night and hair washing night. The fire was stoked up to a glowing red and whilst my mother collected soap and towels. My father carried in the large tin bath which hung outside the kitchen door. It was filled with hot water and after undressing we were allowed to splash about in it for a time. We were washed with a flannel and a tablet of Pears Soap which was a luxury. Our hair was then washed and I used to love it when my mother lifted us out, wrapped a towel around us and lulled by the warmth of the fire, she leaned us against her knees and rubbed our hair dry. There was such a feeling of love and security. It took quite a long time to dry our hair as it was long and there were no hair dryers in those days.

When it was dry, we were put into our clean nighties, given a bowl of Quaker Oats and sent to bed. By this time we were sleepy and contented and ready for sleep. I can't think how

The Chapel ladies cricket team reached a high standard in local competition.

tired our parents must have been as both of them must have had a very heavy day.

When the factory hooter sounded at noon on Saturdays, it meant the end of the working week and there was a relaxed air in the town. Instead of the usual hurry to get home for the mid-day meal and back again to work before the hooter went at the end of the dinner break, men and women sauntered up the street in groups, laughing and talking together.

My father, Arthur Bramwell, was a slater and plasterer and employed three or four men, depending on how busy he was. On a Saturday afternoon the men who worked for him came to the yard to collect their wages, leaning against or sitting on the low stone wall, chatting together or teasing us as we played in the yard. It was an easier day in the house. We usually had a large meat pie from Miss Brocklehurst's shop, which was hot and delicious with chips from Mrs. Marsh's chip shop up the road.

After dinner my father used to clean and polish his boots, change into a suit and in the Summer time be ready with the men and their wives to go to the cricket field. All the villages around, and as far away as Hyde had teams with a very high standard of play. There was keen competition and on the days Chapel played Hayfield, Dove Holes or New Mills, the ground would be packed.

The field was set in the most beautiful area. There were no houses nearby and the view from there, looking across the valley towards Combs Moss and South Head was beautiful and would be hard to beat anywhere in the country. On the day they played Chapel, Hyde players' wives and children came along just to enjoy the scenery.

As I have said, the standard of play was high but one player should be mentioned for his outstanding ability. That was Alf Lomas whom everyone said should have been playing for England.

Sunday was the day when fathers took charge of the elder children whilst mothers prepared the Sunday lunch, which was the highlight of the week, the meal that the family sat

The general view of the breathtaking countryside from Chapel's cricket ground, photographed in the 1940s.

down to together. It usually consisted of roast beef, baked potatoes and two vegetables, followed by rice pudding and apple pie.

As you walked down the street, every house would be exuding a smell of roasting meat, cooked in a side oven of a Yorkshire Range - something that could never be beaten by any modern contraption.

On Saturday nights mothers would have prepared special outfits for the children to wear on Sundays. Hair had to be curled with strips of rag and rolled up so that it would be curly for Sunday. It was very uncomfortable to sleep in rags, but the result next morning was well worth the torture. It was every child's craving to have curly hair because only then would children be considered pretty. Fathers would take their children to visit grandparents on Sunday mornings. We had a grandmother who lived too far away, so much to our pleasure we were taken over the road to Garlick's stables, where we would watch the horses being fed and groomed or play with Garlick's children in the field at the back of the stables. My father often got into trouble when we came home in a dishevelled condition.

If we were having roast lamb for dinner, we usually had to call at Uncle Peter's house, at the top of Church brow, to beg a bunch of mint from his garden to make mint sauce. Many families had sons who were members of the Town Band. The sounds of boys practising the cornet, trombone or deep bass would be heard through the open doors on a Sunday morning.

In the afternoon we were packed off to Sunday school whilst our parents enjoyed the luxury of dozing or reading the Sunday papers in the sitting room. This was furnished with the most treasured possessions, and, invariably, there would be an aspidistra plant. Only at weekends and special occasions was this room used.

Sunday tea was also a bit of a do. A white tablecloth, edged with crochet work was used and best cups and saucers and dishes. There would possibly be home boiled ham with, in summer,

A Sunday evening walk to the Beehive Inn, at Combs, was almost a ritual for many families.

lettuce grown in the garden and tomatoes from my father's greenhouse. This was followed by home made cakes and invariably fruit and custard.

In the evening, if my mother did not go to church, we would do what was almost a ritual for many families: Go for a walk over the level as far as the Beehive Inn. You were sure to meet lots of people you knew and spend considerable time chatting with them.

One thing people looked forward to on certain evenings in the Summer was the parade and hymn singing of the churches sermons. People wore their best clothes, usually new for the occasion and we children more often than not had a new straw hat trimmed with ribbon and artificial flowers.

There was always a bit of a spread for tea as families visited on this special day. My mother's sisters and cousins were sure to be there, especially if it was the Wesleyan Sermons, as this was grudgingly admitted that this was the most colourful turnout of the Church Sermons. I must admit that there were many peevish remarks passed on the ladies new outfits as they passed by with banners blowing in the wind and smart footwork in time to the band.

My mother's family were Congregationalists and as I have already said there was no love lost between denominations. Church members would sing hymns at the workhouse then in the Market Place before returning to their Church.

CHAPTER

~ 8 ~

NEIGHBOURS

Three of our close neighbours were very special to me. Mam Ford was one. Until I was about 12 years old, Mam Ford's cottage was my second home. I could go there whenever I wanted and be sure of a warm welcome. I called her "Mam Ford" and she called me "our Midge". The cottage had two large rooms downstairs and two bedrooms. The stairs went up from the kitchen as was usual in small cottages. There was a stair door shutting them off from the kitchen. The living room had cottage antique furniture and china. Everywhere was polished and scrubbed. It was always shining, warm and comfortable.

There was a large Yorkshire range which glowed with a coal fire. This was surrounded by a cast iron frame and mantlepiece which was painted brown. On the mantlepiece, as in most cottages, the tea caddy was kept in a jar. There was a clock with a painted face and at each end venetian red vases with sparkling lustres hanging from the rims.

At one side of the range was an iron well. It had a hinged lid. This was filled frequently with cold water. As the fire was glowing all day long it provided a constant supply of hot water. How often have I seen Mam Ford slip her arms out of her blouse sleeves, then, with the blouse hanging out of her skirt at the back, take a ladle can, dip it into the water in the well, then carry it to the kitchen sink and empty it into an enamel bowl.

She would then take a piece of flannel, cut a wedge from a bar of white windsor soap, dip the flannel into the hot water, rub it well with soap then begin to lather her arms and neck. I was fascinated by the black corsets she wore. She was so thin with no shape to control, but her stays reached up under her armpits. They were stiffened with whale bone and there was a hollow all the way round her as they were at least two or three inches too big. She looked as if she was standing in a flower pot! Then she would pull the corsets forward and wash down as far as she could reach in front. This washing at the sink was a usual procedure as there were no bathrooms in the cottages.

Mam Ford was the nicest person you could ever wish to meet. So plain to look at and about five foot tall. Her little wrinkled face was a brownish colour (she could have been Romany) but her eyes were bright blue and always twinkling. Her thin hair slightly grey, was drawn up tightly into a small knob onto the top of her head. She had three children, Ernest, Sally and Herbert. She loved them dearly and along with her husband "Dad Ford" (a quiet shy man) they were the most contented family you could wish to know.

They were not too poor, as Dad Ford, along with other members of his family were painters and decorators, and got plenty of work in the big houses locally. This meant they could have small luxuries which were denied less well off families in our street. For instance, Erbie's pigeon loft must have cost quite, a bit and of all luxuries, Erbie had a gramophone with a huge pink horn. I used to love listening to his records, "Little Billy Williams" and "Three Cheers for the Red, White and Blue".

I remember well and still sing songs I learnt then, about Billy Williams finding a penny in the garden and buying a packet of Woodbines, which he smoked with dire results. Erbie also had a bike which was a rare thing in Chapel. His mother seemed to deny him nothing and as things turned out, she must have been so glad he had these few luxuries in his short life.

I never saw Mam Ford dressed in a colour. Always in black and I cannot think she ever had new clothes. Sometimes she would take us for a walk over the fields or on a Sunday we would visit her relatives on Plumpton Farm, Bagshaw. For these occasions she wore a large black straw hat trimmed with satin bows, possibly bought at some time for a funeral.

I think mostly of the winter evenings spent at Mam Ford's as, during the summertime, we were playing in the fields in the evening. I usually went down to their cottage at about six o'clock. My father would stand at the gate to see that I was safe, as the gas lights were not very bright and hardly penetrated across the street. I would knock at the door, and hear Sally say "that will be our Midge at the door".

Some evenings we played dominoes on the big square table which was covered with a floral oil cloth. The canary, whose cage hung on the wall over the kitchen door, would sing loudly all the time. He loved company. Sally and Mam Ford would call to him occasionally. He would listen with his head on one side.

There seemed to be lots more house flies in those days. The ones that escaped from the fly papers hanging from the gas lights or beams became dozey at nights and settled on the ceiling or the oil cloth on the table. We were ready for them, with our rolled papers, and smote each one as it settled. We then picked up our victim by its legs and put it on our side of the table. At the end of the evening we counted our loot for the night.

We passed our time some nights sitting round the table with newspapers and scissors, cutting them into squares to use as toilet paper in the W.C. at the top end of the garden. Holes were made in the corners and string threaded through to hang on the nail provided. The W.C. was at the extreme end of the garden. There was a little window looking out onto the field and occasionally one would be scared by a cow mooing outside or an inquisitive one looking in at the window. It was a scarey adventure going there at night in the dark. Sally used to take me. I gripped her hand when I could, but she was usually shading the candle she carried with her free hand.

Sally would at times, take her crochet work out of the top draw of the chest, unwrap it from the white linen cloth, which was then spread on the table. Most families had one or more daughters who could do this beautiful work. The patterns were most intricate and often the lace was eight inches or more deep. It was made to go round the edges of linen table clothes, but narrow pieces were crocheted for chemises or the edges of pillow cases.

The table cloth would probably have been embroidered before by hand. There was beautiful work done and also great competition among the young women. Nowadays, these crochet edged table cloths are fetching high prices in the antique shops.

Next door to Mam Ford lived Mr. and Mrs. Pell with their three children. They also were kind and very pleasant people. Mr. Pell had a beard and looked like King George V. He was a signal man on the Midland Railway. Every day he was seen off to work by Mrs. Pell waving from the doorway. He carried a wicker basket which had a lid fastened with an iron skewer. This contained his food. He usually carried a garden fork or spade, as most men had a little garden on the banking by the signal box where they grew flowers. They were very competitive and all the way down the line to Manchester in the summer time, these little gardens were a delight. There was keen competition as to who had the most colourful flowers each year.

The next cottage was let furnished in the summer and some visitors enjoyed Chapel so much they bought houses and settled here.

In the corner house next to the shop lived the Slack family. They had two children, Ada and George. Mrs. Slack was a prim, plump woman with lovely curly hair and she helped with confinements and laying out. She was considered a bit of a "swank" about her cooking ability. Sometimes snied remarks were made by neighbours, especially when she helped with the catering for the Freemasons' Dinner, which was held in the Town Hall across the road.

She made trifles "all jelly" the neighbours used to say, vindictively. These she carried across the street, uncovered, and she would stop to speak to anyone she met so she could show them off - or so it was said! It was a pity she had this weakness as she was a very pleasant and generous woman and always found time for the children.

Mr. Slack was one of my favourite people. He always smiled and had time to play with us for a few minutes whenever he saw us. He wore heavy iron shod shoes and a leather apron. He looked after the horses belonging to Mr. J.A. Garlick who had a furniture removing business with huge vans pulled by two or three horses.

In the summer when the plants were in full bloom, Mrs. Slack and Mam Ford would take us over Park Road to the Target Field and gather burnet to make wine. They would both be wearing their black straw hats and perpetual aprons which were worn from getting up in the morning until bed time. I think the apron was a badge of honour to the hard working British housewife. You would be considered improperly dressed without an apron. For Sunday tea-time a white one, usually tucked and frilled, was taken out of the top drawer of the chest and fastened with a broad tie at the back. This was done almost with reverence, as if it was in respect of the Sabbath.

These excursions to gather burnet was something we looked forward to in our summer holidays. We set off with our baskets in a small group along Park Road, a dusty limestone road, with fields on either side of it. Immediately after crossing the bridge was a hedge then a stile and a stone-flagged path leading to the Target field where the volunteer soldiers and the Sherwood Foresters 6th Battalion practiced their shooting. There was a company of Sherwood Foresters based in Chapel at one time. The target was a very high solid stone structure standing in the middle of the field. In front of it was an open space then a high sloping bank where the soldiers lay to take aim with their rifles. Unfortunately, the Target Wall has recently been dismantled. It must have been built about 200 years ago.

The Target field was a great attraction for us. In the Spring the open part of the target became water logged and attracted lots of frogs. We could hardly wait for the frog spawn to appear. At the first sighting we were over there with our jars to collect some. This we put into larger vessels and as the tadpoles appeared we went regularly to the target to get the water for them which would be natural to their development.

It was fascinating to watch the tadpoles turn into little frogs and as this happened we took them back to the Target which was their natural environment.

The Target field was a treasure house of wild flowers and grasses. We knew few of the flowers by their botanical names but we knew the bank where "ladies slipper" and wild thyme grew, the damp places where we could find celandines, the swampy areas for marsh marigolds, the special bank where violets grew and on rare occasions we found wild orchids.

The burnet heads were a lovely dark purple colour and stood out well amongst the more delicate flowers. I'm afraid our minds often wandered from our task and I for one used to pick some shivering glass to take home to my mother.

When our baskets were full we would sit on the bank by the stile to rest, usually making daisy chains or chasing butterflies. At home, the purple heads were stripped from the burnet and boiled with sugar to make wine which was fermented with yeast.

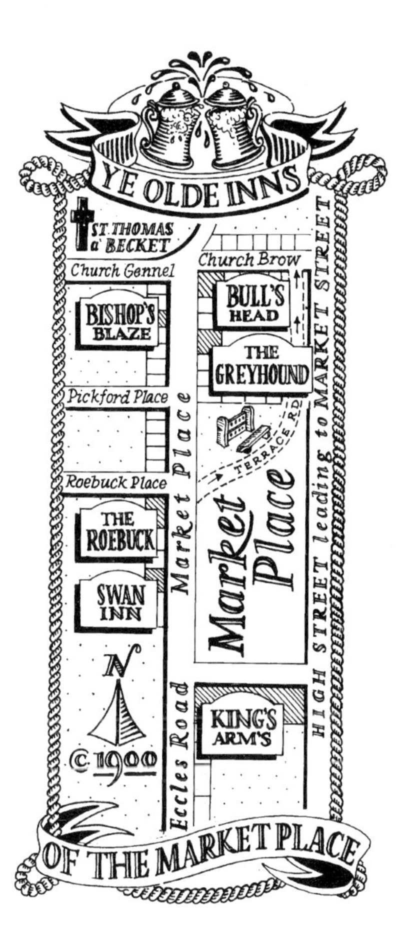

CHAPTER
~ 9 ~

THE INNS OF THE MARKET PLACE

I love the Market Place, the Church Brow and Terrace Road. In spite of a macadam strip and so many cars parked there nowadays. As I walk toward the Church I can feel the still quiet atmosphere I knew as a child. There has been little change in the buildings which are mellow with age. I marvel at the setts which cover the ground and try to imagine loads of stone brought from the quarries and tipped there. Pieces would be chosen and trimmed by hand to fit onto each other. They would be worked by local men, all of them expert by practice. Their tools would be simple hammers, chisels and more likely than not something invented and made by themselves. They would be poorly paid and worked long hours whatever the weather. Often, they would get a sack, push one corner into the other making a shape like a pixie hat and would put their head in this shape and the rest of the sack would cover their shoulders and back, keeping them warm and dry.

Originally there were six inns in the Market Place. ***The Bull's Head***, with a stone sculpture of a bull's head high over the front door. Thank goodness, the mounting stone and steps remain. The story goes that one dark night - a noted young man came out of the pub in a drunken state. He climbed the steps to mount his horse. Unfortunately, the horse moved at the vital moment and he fell to his death.

I remember one winter when snow slid off the roof bringing the gutter with it. It caught the carving and broke the horns off. A new one was created by a stone-mason called Hamer who lived at New Smithy.

A few yards away there used to be another inn called ***The Greyhound***. It is now a house. Across the other side was ***Bishop's Blaze Inn***. There is a dental surgery there now. If you look on the pavement you will see an iron grille which was the entrance to the cellar where the

The "Lilly Ground" in the Market Place once had a lamp (right) supported by a decorative wrought iron stand set on a large plinth of stone. Even today I love the Market Place and as I walk towards the Church I can still feel its quiet atmosphere.

barrels were stored. The next one was ***The Roebuck***, kept by the Barlows and then ***The Swan Inn***, which I remember well. It is now the post office. There was a flight of stone steps and an iron handrail to the door.

The Kings Arms is much as it has always been, except that the front entrance was on the High Street. It was elegant, with a stone sculptured archway that can still be seen against the wall. Stone steps went up to the door and there were brass railings on each side. The inn did a roaring trade on Market days catering with roast beef sandwiches and strong ale. It is sad that as the traffic increased, for safety's sake, the elegant High Street entrance to the King's Arms had to be closed.

At the top of the hill the road was very narrow with no pavement on the Market side. From the main road there were two flights of steps up to the Market Place. They were beautifully designed to meet the level of the Market. Coming up the hill was another entrance. On the right hand side was a curved flight of stone steps again wide and narrowing at the top. There was an iron handrail with iron bollards to hold it. The left hand side was paved like the market. This was for barrows and handcarts.

These entrances were all attractive and I am sure there had been caring thought before they were built. How different they were to the steep and ugly steps that replaced them. How pleased I am that the more recent renovations in the Market Place have been carried out with such care and understanding.

Where the War Memorial now stands there used to be a large plinth of stone. In the centre was a lamp supported by a decorative wrought iron stand. It was always called The Lilly Ground. I often wish I knew why. The Stocks in my youth had the original woodwork. What a pity it could not have been preserved!

The Market Place was the venue for all meetings that were relevant to the town. Hymn singing after the Sermons parades, political meetings and the Cattle Market every Thursday.

The Market Place, the centre of town life, was the setting for the ox roast on July 7, 1925, to mark the 700th anniversary of the Parish Church. The Rev. Norman Bennett cut the first slice.

The very special event for children was Bonfire Night. The Market Place would be packed with parents and children. A group of local men collected firewood, branches of trees and any boxes or paper which people wanted destroyed. All this was assembled in the centre and with experience, built to be sure it would kindle and burn well. Of course, it always did and it was a great treat to be there to watch the fire grow into a blazing mass. It was certainly a most exciting sight to see the flames and all the people and the Market Place in the glow of the fire. We were given pennies to buy fireworks from Hibbert's shop, spa sparklers, jumpjacks and cannons. They mostly cost a penny. Winnie and I and the children who lived near the brewery thought ourselves lucky on Bonfire Night, as Mr. Simpson from the brewery got plastering laths from my father to make rockets. I don't know how he did it, but he used gunpowder and they were always a great success. They were very big and went high into the sky. I was always a bit frightened of them. We knew that when we went home there would be homemade treacle toffee and parkin for us. It was a wonderful scene and, as the fire burned low, people put potatoes in the embers to roast.

For Bonfire Night, the Market Place would be packed by parents and children.

CHAPTER

~ 10 ~

THE LOCAL SHOPS

In Eccles Road where it meets the Market Place was a large Victorian house. Mrs. Pink and her family lived there. Mr. Pink had been a previous vicar at the Parish Church. The Pink family was much respected and loved in the town. There were two boys and two girls who integrated well in all the local activities, especially the girls, Mary and Connie. Connie was a great sports woman. She formed the ladies cricket team. She herself played as good a game as any man and trained her team until they were almost unbeatable round the district. Many of the local villages, as far as New Mills, had a ladies team and there was keen competition.

The first shop on the Market was kept by a refined lady called Miss Righton. She sold greeting cards and stationery. At the back of the shop was a small room which she had as a library. The books were mostly romantic novels and she did a fair trade lending them out at two pence per week.

The next shop was a shoe shop owned by Mr. and Mrs. Slack. They had three sons who were cobblers and had a workshop in the Wakes field near the New Inn. The younger son Freddy, who sadly had a hunch back, served mostly in the shop. There were two windows, always looking dismal. One for ladies shoes, all very substantial to attract farmers wives no doubt, the other one displayed mens working boots and shoes. Inside in the centre of the back wall, was a flight of steps with an opening at the top which was draped with a faded red velvet curtain trimmed with red bobbles down each side. A stranger entering the shop would be slightly shocked as the curtain was pulled aside at the vision of Freddy standing there with his mop of blonde curls. They were soon put at ease, however, by Freddy's charm and intelligence.

Freddy was a very talented water colour painter and his brother Herbert was a gifted engineer and artist. As I have said, they had a workshop in the Wakes field and when the horse roundabout was in action at the fair during Wakes Week they had an opportunity to study the workings of it. They used their knowledge to build a model merry-go-round which was about several feet in radius and perfect in every detail.

Working for many hours with another Chapel engineer, Harold Pearce, they built the merry-go-round from metal, with every horse in perfect proportion and painted in different designs. There were twisted brass hand holds and in the centre, pictures of painted ladies who held cymbals which were made to beat time with the music. There were steps from outside onto the working platform. The whole thing worked to perfection. As the engine started, the music came on and the horses glided up and down as the whole roundabout turned round. It was a thing of genius and eventually was entered for an international competition in London and won first prize. Years later it was used on BBC television as an introduction to achildren's programme *Whirligig.* We were very proud of it!

Slack's model roundabout, perfect in every detail.

Old Mr. Slack, their father, was a strange man. He always wore a large black hat and long black coat. He always carried a Bible from which he prophesied the end of the world.

Then under a glass veranda there was a greengrocer called Mr. Partridge and a plumber called Mr. Leckanby. Across from them was a butcher's shop called Hyde & Co., originally owned by two brothers, Joseph and Ebenezer Hyde. It was said, and it was true, that Ebenezer the book-keeper, hibernated from October until April. He retired to bed and carried on working from there, wearing his top hat to protect him from the cold!

In 1905 the business and premises were taken over by Mr. Marshall who continued it until his retirement. Stanley House as it was called was always one of my favourite buildings in Chapel.

Nearer the Church, next to what had been the Greyhound Inn was a shoe and cobblers business kept by the Woodcock family. Old Mr. Woodcock was a small, kindly man and his son Frank was more than 6ft tall, completely bald and with very large teeth. Wearing his black cobblers apron he resembled Frankenstein. I was always a bit afraid of him.

The Church Brow fortunately is much as it always was. At the bottom of the brow was Mr. Potts' joinery shop. He made most of the coffins that were needed in the town. In the first cottage on Terrace Road lived Teddy Ford. He was a small man with red hair and was always immaculately turned out. His attire consisted of breeches, black jacket with brass buttons and a tall hat decorated with a cockade on the side. He had a closed cab and a landau which he drove for hired fares and did a very good trade at weddings and funerals. He had a stable on Eccles Road where he kept his horse.

His carriages were always in immaculate condition and there is a story of a booking he once had. It was arranged that he would meet Mr. Hyde off the train at the North West station one evening. He had a wedding booked for the next day and had cleaned and polished the cabs to perfection. It rained during the afternoon and he was loath to use the

This photograph of Church Brow was taken in the 1940s, but would have looked much the same in the early 1900s. There were the small cottage gardens outside some of the houses. And thankfully - it is still much the same today.

cab. He did meet Mr. Hyde off the train but on foot and with an umbrella!

The Nobles, who were landlords of the Kings Arms, also had vehicles for hire and there was plenty of trade for both of them. They lived a strange life but were always friendly and entertaining to talk to. Their father had been a carter, mostly moving stone from the quarries. It was said locally that if the weather was bad the sons used to say "It isner fit t'turn a dog out, thou'll have to go th'self Father". Sam Longson used to say another bad weather greeting in Chapel was : "The dead are missing nowt today, Sam!"

Next to the Town Hall lived the Dawe family. Mr. Dawe was the Stationmaster on the Midland Railway Station. He was a dignified man, as his position required. Mr. and Mrs. Dawe had a daughter called Cissie who had a millinery shop in the front room of their house. She was a very precise young woman who had never been allowed to mix with other young people in the town. She was supposedly "A young lady". Her whole life seemed to be helping her mother to clean the house to excess and serve her customers in the shop.

At precisely nine o'clock every morning Cissie would fling back the green curtains at the back of the shop window then without pause put six tall hat stands in two precise rows, place a hat on each one and lastly give a sharp twist to each one as if to say "Behave yourself or else…" before she closed the curtains again. I always thought the window display looked like guards on duty outside Buckingham Palace.

Milliners sold decorations for the hats that they made from buckram shapes. Buckram was a coarse cloth stiffened with size, then moulded into a variety of shapes of hats. You chose the style that suited you then from bundles of straw, which was about half an inch wide, the hat was covered, then stitched in circles beginning at the crown.

There were lots of decorations to choose from, artificial flowers and bunches of fruit were very popular. Ribbon of course, was always used, often to make a tail hanging from the back of the hat. You chose the colour you wanted from rolls of ribbon with paper between, looking like a toilet roll. In this way it was kept clean and uncreased. Veils were sold in various lengths and widths, as they were put over the brim of the hat, pulled down over the face and under the chin, then pinned to the back of the hat.

I have described a few of the shops in Chapel, but the others also had character. I think this stemmed from the fact that the shops were attached to the home and family and were more or less neighbours of their customers. There were no isolated shopping areas, all of them mingled with the cottages in the street.

Down the street at the beginning of Town End was a small grocery shop kept by Mrs. Frith. She was a widow and had three sons and three daughters. They were all adult and went out to work. The shop was small and dark and always had a strong smell of paraffin which was kept in a tank at the back of the shop. She did a fair trade as most people had oil lamps in their houses and came there for paraffin and bought groceries as well.

As Mam Ford's family made a great fuss of me, so did the Friths, always welcoming my sister and me to their house. Mrs. Frith's husband had been a miller and was always referred to as "Dusty Frith". They also had a small holding at the back of the house. There was a shippon and a barn where a few cows were kept. These grazed in a large field behind.

I used to love going to the Friths with Winnie. There was always something interesting to do. Going with Patty to bring the cows in at milking time, I remember once from the field seeing South Head and asking Patty what was on the other side. "It's a foreign country," she said. "They don't speak English, they have a language of their own. It's called Scotland."

I enjoyed helping Mrs. Frith getting the hen food together on a winter night. She boiled potato peeling she had saved and whilst they were still hot mixed meal in with them, stirring it round and round in a bucket. The hens screeching and flapping their wings trying to get onto the rim of the bucket, then a fighting mass of feathers and beaks when it was emptied into the stone trough.

CHAPTER
~ 11 ~

STARTING SCHOOL

I started at the Church School when I was five years old. My first teacher was called Miss Middleton. She was a pleasant person and we were all happy in her class. One of the first things I can remember in my school life was the class being taken out onto the street and put in line along the edge of pavement. The street was full of people clapping and cheering. In the distance a band was playing. Soon it came in sight, followed by a regiment of men marching smartly in time to the music. We were told to wave our handkerchiefs and cheer. I did not know why so many people were crying until we were back in our class, and Miss Middleton explained to us that a war had started and the marching men had all volunteered to go and fight for England. The procession turned up to the station where a train was waiting to take them to Derby where they would begin their training.

As the years went by I had to learn what sadness really was, also the reality of the 1914 war when so many of those men marching and many more besides, were killed and wounded which brought great sadness to so many families in the town.

In my second year at school I moved up into Miss Wilkie's class. She was a horrible old woman and as I have already mentioned would walk around the classroom with a cane in her hand, using it often. I was too afraid of Miss Wilkie to learn much in her class and at the end of the year I failed the test to go up into Standard Two. My parents objected and I was given another test which I passed and was then free of Miss Wilkie and went into a higher class.

I soon made new friends, gained confidence and began to enjoy school. My new teacher was called Miss Ford. Like most of the teachers she was quite old and wore a red wig, possibly to hide her grey hair. We were all fascinated by it, as it was always slipping to one side and being pushed back into place with a pencil. She was strict in class, but fair, and she

With my classmates at Chapel Church School, now Chapel Infants School - 1913.
I am third from right in the second row.

made her lessons interesting.

Facilities in the school were meagre. Heating in the class rooms was by iron hot water pipes against one wall. The only fire was a small one next to the teacher's desk. We were never warm enough and had to wear, in winter, thick woollen stockings and jerseys. Desks were in rows of six, with an attached backless form to sit on. They were very uncomfortable and we were reprimanded if we did not sit with a straight back.

We had books for reading lessons and writing books for composition. Otherwise we used slates and usually pieces of broken slate pencils. As part of arithmetic we all stood up in class and chanted our "times tables" until we knew them by heart, which I must admit has been useful to me for the rest of my life.

We had sewing lessons mostly to teach us the art of darning and patching. As so called 'practise', the teacher brought her husband's old shirts and underwear to repair. When finished, she used to sell them at a shilling a garment. I was never popular as my mother would not let us buy anything.

I was fortunate that one teacher in the senior class was interested in art and I learnt quite a lot from her. She did not teach us how to draw in pencil. All we had were small pieces of pastel. The only subjects to copy were leaves or flowers and, in winter, twigs off the bare trees. Our drawing books had coloured paper, interleaved with tissue paper to keep the pastel from smudging. I still have my book of drawings done nearly 80 years ago and will always treasure it.

Some of the children had long distances to travel to get to school and as there was no transport, they had to walk to school and back, be it rain or, in winter, snow. As there were no means of drying their clothes, these children often went home in them still wet from the morning. No wonder there were so many bad coughs and colds! As most of the children wore long woollen stockings there was, in wet weather, always a smell of wet wool drying as they sat in the class room. No lunch was provided. Children brought sandwiches to be eaten in the class room in winter but in the cloakroom or in the school yard in summer.

Lavatories were wooden planks with a hole in the centre. There was no toilet roll provided and no chain to pull. Until you got used to it, it was a frightening experience as water flushed periodically through the whole length of the lavatory. The boys had an open urinal at the side of the toilets with no privacy as the girls waited their turn. They often had an interested audience as the boys competed to see which boy could pee the highest!

Once a year a doctor and a nurse came to the school and gave all the children a medical examination. Mothers were allowed to be there and it was a chance for them to ask questions or be told if their child was suffering from any complaint of which they were unaware. If so, how serious it was and if it needed treatment. This was a very good service.

Periodically a nurse came to inspect children's hair for head lice. This was a very common thing with all children having long hair, which in many cases was not washed for quite long periods of time. My mother combed our hair with a fine tooth comb every Friday night at bath time to be sure we were free of them.

With the exception of the headmistress, none of the teachers were certificated. Even so, we were well taught as they were all dedicated to their work.

When we were thirteen years old, and if our parents wanted us to go to secondary school, we sat a scholarship examination. If we passed, we went by choice either to Cavendish High School for Girls in Buxton or New Mills Secondary School for boys and girls. My parents had no faith in my ability to pass, so I was entered as a private pupil at Cavendish, but I surprised them all by passing a local Charity Scholarship called the Dixen and Kirk, which over the years seemed to pass into oblivion.

When I started at Cavendish my lifestyle changed. It was the beginning of a new life for me. Needless to say, the best part of school life was the Christmas, Easter and Summer

Holidays. Whichever holiday, there was always something exciting to look forward to, mostly over the park at Longson's Farm, or in the meadow. As soon as the Christmas holiday started, we were up in the Target Field finding the holly bush with the most berries on it. We broke pieces off to take home to decorate the house. We then went on to the railway bank to break a branch off a young fir tree to use as a Christmas tree.

We put this in the corner of the sitting room and with a few coppers our mother gave us, bought a length of tinsel to decorate it. Silver paper was precious and we saved every scrap and made it into stars which covered cut out cardboard shapes to hang from the branches.

The kitchen that week was heavenly! My mother mixing the Christmas cake and we in anticipation of scraping out the delicious mixture she left in the bowl. Mince pies cooking and puddings boiling, then helping to decorate the cake when it was iced. We were well worked up for Father Christmas coming.

Stockings were hung up and we were thrilled next morning to find what to us was marvellous. An apple and an orange and some nuts. Usually a stick of plasticine, some crayons, a drawing book, a string of beads and a packet of sweets, but always one or two books. One year I was thrilled to find a doll, which was a rare treat. I kept this doll for a long time, until its body burst and all the sawdust came out. Its eyes went into its head and its wig came off. In the end there was nothing to play with.

I was told that I could not have a new one until my birthday which was nearly a year away so I had a bright idea...Recessed in the thick wall of the kitchen was a small window overlooking the yard. Every night a candle was lit and put in there so that when we went to the lavatory which was across the yard, we could leave the door open to see the light and not be afraid.

Every night I made a nick at the top of the candle which made the tallow run down the side. I scraped it off frequently so it was not noticed. After a time I had quite a sizeable lump of tallow. I then warmed it until it was pliable and modelled it into a baby doll. I had just had some new slippers which were always sold in a box. Another useful collectors item! I made this into a bed with bits and pieces I had found and standing the box lid at the back of the box to make the bed head.

All this was done secretly and when I wanted to play with it I took it under the sitting room table which had a long red cloth reaching to the ground.

One night my father said: "What are you doing under there?"

I said I was playing. He asked: "What with?" I said: "My doll".

"But you haven't got a doll. Let me see it". I showed it to him and tears came into his eyes. "If you want a doll as badly as that," he said, "you shall have one".

The next day my mother went to Walker's shop and bought a beautiful one with eyes that closed and the body was made of kid.

I still have that doll after 80 years but I never loved it as much as the little tallow one I made myself from the candle.

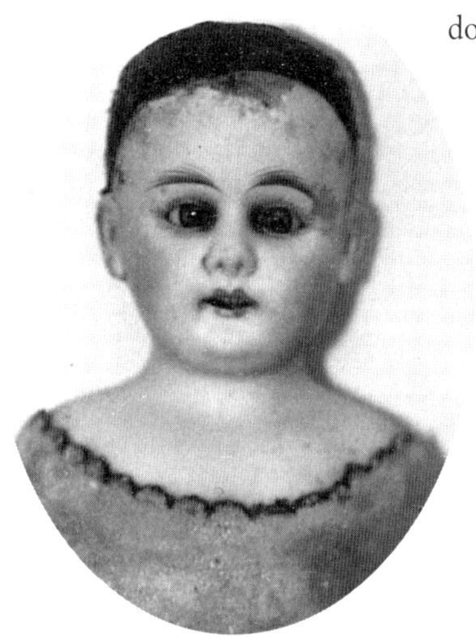

Once bearing a beautiful wig and dress, this is my treasured doll today.

CHAPTER
~ 12 ~

WHEN WINTER CAME

In my childhood winters were much more severe than they are today. We children were always excited when the first snow flakes began to fall, especially if it was near to Christmas time. That is how we thought Christmas should be, but it must have been a nightmare for adults when the snow got deep and drifted. Sledges were used for moving goods and taking fodder to sheep that had been put in folds nearer the farm at the first sign of bad weather. There were no such things as wellingtons and men wore leggings if they had any, otherwise, they wrapped lengths of sacking torn from a bag to wrap around their legs to keep dry and warm.

Usually drifts were so high that it was impossible to walk up the street and people had to dig a way out of their houses and through the drifts if possible to get to work. We had to stay away from school until the footpaths could be cleared by men pushing a contraption with two handles like a wheelbarrow, but coming to a point at the front, making a wedge shape to cut through the drifts.

As soon as part of the yard was cleared, we were out feeding the birds and making a snowman. We put pieces of old woollen socks over our shoes so that we would not slip and hurt ourselves. One danger we were warned about was of thick snow sliding off the roofs, bringing guttering down with it. Quite a few people were hurt every winter by this.

In February, we usually had very hard frosts which froze Combs Lake. This was a marvellous expanse of ice. People made the most of it. Once the ice was pronounced safe, many skaters in the town flocked over there, especially at weekends. Parents took children to slide or sledge. It was lovely to see so many people you knew enjoying themselves. At night, fires were lit on the banks and lanterns put about which made a lovely scene.

My father outside our house on Market Street (just opposite from the Town Hall) during a severe winter.

Ada pulling a sledge.

The worst part of the winter was now to come! When the atmosphere warms up and the thaw sets in, what a dreary sight the streets became. Full of dirty sludge and water that the drains could not take. Brooms were the order of the day as husbands and wives did their best to clear the filth and water.

When the streets, yards and gardens were beginning to look clean again, there was a small but pleasant surprise when in the gardens from the last bit of snow, snowdrops were found heralding the spring!

In the winter, there was a well supported football team. The field was over Park Road, the pitch was rough pasture and there were no changing rooms or pavilion. Players changed at the King's Arms Hotel and walked down the street to the football field. Supporters stood along the sidelines and there was barely a space to be found. At half time, coffee was made at the King's Arms, carried down the street in two pails by George Nall and given to the players to drink. Star players were Johnnie and Bobbie Noble who lived at the King's Arms.

Unbelievable as it may seem, films were shown on Saturday afternoon and evenings. A Mr. and Mrs. Taylor, who I think came from New Mills, hired the Constitutional Hall on Saturdays to show films. I don't know how the projector worked as there was no electricity in Chapel. I can only think it was worked from batteries. It was worked from the top of the ceiling at the entrance porch.

All seats were wood and fastened together on long rows. At the back there was a row of arm chairs, only used for evening shows. They cost a shilling and the rest were ninepence. We paid a penny in the afternoon. It was a very exciting. Eccles Road would be crowded with children waiting for opening time. A pianist, assisted in the evening by a boy with a kettle drum, played loud, angry music at the violent scenes then at the romantic parts she played sentimental "twaddle". Films were mostly American with lots of cowboys and gangsters. There was always one that was "continued next week".

I remember one film which frightened me very much and I could not get it out of mind. Iyt ended one Saturday with the heroine left tied to a railway line with a train puffing towards her. My mother must have had something special on the next Saturday for, in spite of my fears, she made me go to see the next episode, saying "Take your doll and if it gets nasty look at it"! All turned out well when the heroine was rescued by the hero.

Another asset to Chapel, the Mens' Institute, was used a lot on Saturday nights. There was a billiard table upstairs and a card and reading room downstairs. Also downstairs was a bathroom which members could use for a small charge.

CHAPTER ~ 13 ~

HEALTH AND HYGIENE

Much as I enjoyed the pleasures of my young life, there was much suffering in those days from illnesses caused by lack of hygiene. Fortunately, over the years, this has improved beyond imagination. Cures have been found for infectious diseases, many of which were serious and often fatal. We were lucky in Chapel to have a fever hospital where diphtheria and scarlet fever patients were nursed. Mumps and whooping cough, although highly infectious, were not considered as dangerous and had to be nursed at home - possibly spreading the infection through the whole family.

When I was six years old I caught scarlet fever and had to go into the hospital - which now houses the High Peak Borough Council offices in Hayfield Road. The ambulance was a horse drawn cab which was only used for fever cases. It was kept until needed in an old stone barn in a field which is now part of the Park. When it arrived to take me to hospital my father carried me to it wrapped in a blanket, but when my parents saw the state of the cab they refused to let me go in it. It was covered with green mould and the straw stuffing had been gouged out of the upholstery by rats making a nest. Reluctantly, they let me go when the nurse in charge promised to keep me on her knee all the way. This is one example of the careless lack of hygiene in those days.

We were kept in hospital for six weeks, very poorly but well looked after and comforted by the fact that most of the nurses were local girls. Parents visited at the weekends but could only talk to us through the windows. They brought goodies to eat and a toy to play with. When we were well enough to get up, we sat around a coke-burning stove in the middle of the ward, with rugs on the floor to keep us warm as we played with our toys. We were soon quite well and could walk out in the garden if well wrapped up as it was winter time.

One symptom of scarlet fever was that all your skin peeled off. It was a slow process but until the shedding was complete you could still infect other people. The toughest skin was on your feet and every day we sat on the edge of the bath with our feet soaking in strong soapy water. Then they were rubbed with a pumice stone which was painful. When I finally went home my father shed tears when he saw that my feet were raw and bleeding.

Ten days after my return my sister went into hospital with fever. My parents were certain she caught it from my raw feet!

Consumption, or tuberculosis as it is now called, was a dreaded disease which seemed to be inherited by families. There was no known cure and people died at a young age. In the field behind the fever hospital was a wooden building with a veranda all round. Patients were taken there and slept on the verandas hoping that continual fresh air would help cure them.

A doctor's life was very hard. There were so few telephones, that however far out of town you lived, and even if it was the middle of the night, someone had to walk to the surgery possibly to get a doctor out of bed. He would then either walk or go by bicycle or pony and trap to attend the patient. If medicine was needed, one had to go to the surgery for it. There were no chemists to supply medicine, which was dispensed by the doctor and a charge was made.

Babies were born in the home. Mothers relied on help from neighbours. One or two women who, without training, had acquired skill in delivering babies by being called in to help at a confinement.

Everyone in the town must at some time or another suffered from toothache and many older people had bad teeth which were painful and unsightly. This was no fault of their own as there was no dentist to go to for an extraction or filling. The doctor would extract the tooth but this was always very painful and people preferred to put up with the tooth aching.

When I was about six years old a dentist started to come to Chapel from New Mills and rented a room in a cottage for one day a week. The surgery was in the sitting room. Patients waited their turn in the kitchen, which was always full as no appointments could be made. They always had to wait a long time, with children crying in pain and with fright.

Apparatus used was crude and it always hurt to have a tooth out. The machine he used for filling teeth was made of wood and he used a foot treadle to turn the drill. Fortunately, we little children never had to have a filling. If a tooth ached it was pulled out there and then.

There was not even a district nurse until, as time went by, people subscribed a penny a week to help pay for a resident district nurse. For many ailments there were home made remedies, some of them passed down for generations. One of the oldest known was water from "Nannies Well" on Crossings Road. Its name was derived from a mediaeval saint called Ninian who in ancient times found cures from natural sources.

"Nannies Well" must have been used by so many people that an iron pump with a drinking cup hanging by a chain was put there, then later it was fenced in and a seat provided for people to rest as it was used by people from far and wide. It remains there today.

I don't know what the water was meant to cure, but when I was a small child I suffered from inflamation of my eyes and my father used to take a bottle, fill it with the iron water from the well and my mother bathed my eyes with it several times a day. My eyes must have shown some improvement or they would not have persisted with the treatment.

One horrific so called "cure" for whooping cough should have been condemned as cruelty to children. Families who had children suffering from the complaint arranged to meet with their children at the warming stone on Park Road.

The fathers carrying the children set out to walk over Park Road, then up the Eaves Drive and onward to Dove Holes. They found their way to the quarries, then to the kilns that burnt the limestone. There was red heat from the burning stone and a great deal of smoke coming from it. Each child in turn was lifted by their father and held over the terrifying furnace until, with all their screaming and crying, it was thought they had inhaled enough smoke to help clear the whooping cough. I have never forgotten it. With all those screaming children being carried home whooping and coughing their hearts out. It's a wonder they did not all have a fit. It is an experience that I have never forgotten.

Children were also taken to the gas works on Hayfield Road and held over the coke furnace, as the smoke from it contained tar which was supposed to be a cure for whooping cough.

Many old people were blind, which in many cases was caused by cataracts on the eyes for which no cure was known. How different it is today, when they can be removed and sight restored with only an overnight stay in hospital.

Deafness was also common. Many people thought it was caused by hard wax in the ears. The supposed remedy was to soak a small piece of cotton wool in warm olive oil then push it into the ear, keep it in for a few days, then remove the wax with the round end of a hair pin. If this did not help, then you accepted the fact that you were deaf and had to put up with it.

People who were well off bought an ear trumpet. It was shaped like a cow's horn of which the narrow end fitted into the ear. People shouted through the wide end. It was a very clumsy contraption but there must have been some benefit as many people used them.

For constipation, senna pods were boiled until the water was dark yellow. We were given this to drink at night before we went to bed. There was always a fuss as it had a foul bitter taste. Next morning we knew we had taken it, as we were running to the W.C. so often!

Bread soaked in hot water was made into a poultice to bring boils and abscesses to a head. Comfrey leaves were boiled and wrapped in a cloth to ease the pain of a sprain or rheumatic condition. Powdered brimstone and black treacle were mixed and given by the spoonful to cure an itching rash. A mixture of beef dripping and brown sugar was rubbed on chapped hands to soften the skin.

Most men who worked out of doors in the winter had swollen knuckles which burst into open cracks which were very painful to heal. Many of them, my father included, melted a piece of cobbler's wax in a candle flame and dropped it into the cracks. This eased the pain and sealed the cracks against infection.

To reduce itching, smarting and swelling of chilblains on toes and heels, potato peelings were boiled and, after cooling a while, the mixture was emptied into a bowl in which we soaked our feet. This reduced the inflamation and made our feet much more comfortable.

In our yard there was a large tank that was used for slaking lime. A cart load of burnt limestone from the quarry was tipped into it then it was filled up with water. As the lime dissolved it began to boil until the stone melted and became slurry which, after a few days, sank to the bottom of the tank, leaving about a foot of water on the top. This was covered and kept clean. If anyone burnt or scalded themselves they would come for a helping of this lime water, which was used to bathe the wound to ease the pain and supposedly to heal the wound.

A goose was very popular for Christmas dinner. There was plenty of fat from the carcass and this was always saved and stored in jars, as goose grease was used to rub on the chest to ease the pain and help breathing if you were suffering from bronchitis or had a sore throat.

...a beautiful walk to Chapel Milton on a summer's day...

CHAPTER ~ 14 ~

THE BUILDING OF THE VIADUCT

Another treat we enjoyed during the Summer holiday was being taken to my grandmother's in Chapel Milton. The first treat was calling at Warhurst's confectioners shop on the corner of Hayfield Road. My mother always bought us a large bun with icing and a cherry in the centre. They were delicious but we had to wait until we were off the street before we were allowed to eat them. This meant all the way down Hayfield Road until we were near Stoddart.

Sometimes we went down Hayfield Road and over Stoddart. This was a beautiful walk with cows feeding in the fields of Stoddart Farm which was a group of lovely old buildings. The road was overhung with massive beech trees which in the Spring were a beautiful sight with their bright green leaves and in the Autumn a blaze of gold.

People walked over Stoddart to enjoy the spectacle of the brilliant colours. We usually persuaded our mother to cross the road at the cottages, through a stile and along a path to a flight of steps and onto a bridge.

The bridge crossed the gravity railway line that carried the trucks of limestone from Dove Holes, via Top o' th' Plane, to the Bugsworth Basin. There they were loaded onto the canal barges on their way North by canal. We were thrilled if we could hear a rumbling in the distance, knowing it was well worth while to wait to see the exciting spectacle of the train of wagons passing under the bridge.

At last they came in sight, travelling at speed, swaying and bouncing along. They were controlled by one man, who must have been very brave as he rode on a wheel axle with only a long wooden pole to control the speed. There were lengths of chain along the wagons and to brake he pushed the pole into a link of the chain which shortened it and so applied a

Chapel Milton, looking Northward towards Gorsty Low, with the viaduct (on the left) and the Cross Keys Inn the mid foreground.

brake to the wheels. As this dragon-like monster passed under the bridge the noise was deafening. We were nearly shaken off it. The trucks hurtled on for about a hundred yards, then, looking like a monster out of a fairy story, disappeared into a tunnel as if going into a witches den!

After the hullabaloo of the passing trucks, we were subdued as we went into the sanctuary of Bowden Lane, passing the ruins of the old silk mill and across the road to the old cottages which had once upon a time been the "Drum and Monkey" Inn.

Further along the road we passed the Blouse works and on the right hand side of the lane, where it joins the main road, there was a farm which was also the post officc. The farmer was called Winterbottom and was married to my mother's cousin. We stopped for a chat if any of them were in the farmyard. The main road at this point divided two dams, which provided water for the running of the mill. It was a beautiful old building driven by a water wheel and was called Rag Mill.

The incline plain of the gravity railway at Chapel that carried the trucks of limestone from Dove Holes to the Bugsworth Basin.

My mother took us down the lane to watch the buckets on the wheel, as they scooped water from the dam. The mill, its yard and outbuildings were ancient and beautiful. They should have been preserved.

My grandmother lived in a row of cottages below the new viaducts. At the end of them was the Cross Keys Inn. Before the viaducts were built, my grandparents lived in a cottage near the mill dams. I loved hearing about the life in Milton when the viaducts were being built. In those days the Cross Keys was an ancient inn and at one time was kept by my great grandmother, who was very old and a great character. Apparently she sat in a corner of the old fireplace all day smoking a clay pipe.

My mother lived, or perhaps a truer word would be existed, in Chapel Milton all the years the viaducts were being built. It must have been bedlam with all the noise, filth and movement of horse-drawn carts carrying loads of earth and pulling huge stones from the quarries. She told of the time when the ground was marshy. The builders could not get a firm foundation and for two years pile drivers were in use night and day. The noise was terrific and made sleep almost impossible. When at last a firm foundation was made, the pillars that supported several of the arches were built as deep into the ground as they were high.

...my painting of the amazing construction of the viaducts of Chapel Milton.

When you look at this structure it is difficult to believe that each block has been shaped by a man from a rough boulder of rock using only a hammer and

The Wash, looking up to Bowden Head.

chisel. Each stone had to be a precise size and tongued and grooved to fit each other. They were neatly worked on the outer sides and finished off in the centre with rough chiseling as a decoration. Two holes can still be seen which were made to hold the clamps which gripped and held them in place as they were hauled by crane into place.

The men who fashioned these stones were called bankerhands. They each had their own mark which they incised into the stone so it can almost be said that each stone was autographed. These bankerhands worked out of doors, protected from the weather by makeshift shelters they erected themselves.

It is difficult to assess how many men were employed and where they were fed. They lived in a tin town which was in the fields above Cornheys Farm. How many horses and carts were used carting the stone from the quarries and on the site? There must have been an enormous workforce employed on the actual building of the structure, plus all the men in charge of the horses, working with them and tending to the stabling, feeding and grooming.

All along the Wash Road were the blacksmiths shops. Shoeing the dozens of horses must have been a non-stop job. When the New Smithy Chapel was rebuilt, the smithies were moved closer to Chinley and that is how it became known as "New Smithy" and has retained the name.

At the same time as the viaduct was being constructed the Cowburn Tunnel was being built. All the shale from it was carried by horse and cart to the Wash. This pile became a mountain and an eyesore to the pretty Wash village.

My mother used to tell of an horrific series of accidents that occurred there and caused much distress. The tip became very high but was kept flat on top for the carts to cross. It was firm in the middle but loose shale at the edges. Quite often a horse and cart would be backed to the edge to be emptied. The shale would break loose and give way when the cart was backed to the edge then the cart and horse would fall backwards off the edge, turning upside down as it fell. It must have been a terrible thing to see.

About 20 years ago, I painted a picture which I called John Barber's Dinner. A strange title for an unusual subject. It had a background of open country. The foreground was a stone wall with a grassy bank in front of it. On the bank was a large pile of limestone chippings and on these was a red and white spotted handkerchief. Spread on it were slices of bread and a lump of cheese, an apple, a bottle of cold tea and a pocket knife to cut it with.

I got inspiration for it from a walk with my mother up Castleton Road many years before. We came across a man sitting on a pile of chippings. He was called John Barber and was related to my mother, so we stopped to chat with him. I think I must have been very taken by the scene for it to remain in my mind for so many years.

These loads of stone were tipped at intervals along the roads. Men were employed to work where the stone was tipped to break the stones with a hammer into small pieces. This rubble was used to fill in holes on the road that had been worn by wheels and horses hooves. It must have been a tedious job and in Winter very cold. In some places they had huts to shelter the men.

We were always being taken for walks and if it was to one of the farms belonging to my mother's relatives we were particularly thrilled. We knew we were sure of a warm welcome with plenty of interesting things to see and do. The farms we visited were Bowden Head, Malcoff and Shire Oaks.

Our favourite was Bowden Head. Uncle Humphrey, his son Isaac and two daughters, Clara and Lizzie, lived there. They let us help them feed the pigs, bring the cows in at milking time and feed the hens which I loved as we had to search for nests of eggs where the ones who were going broody laid away. Usually we found them tucked away in the hay barn. They looked so pretty when we moved the sitting hen that it seemed to be a sin to disturb her.

Winnie and I loved searching the fields for mushrooms. We took a large square red and white spotted neckerchief to carry them in. The men who went mushrooming just after dawn broke always carried them bundled up in such a neckerchief, so it did not seem right to carry wild mushrooms in a basket.

Bowden Head Farm was a delight. It had a stone paved porch and short passage which led into the living room kitchen. The ceiling was low and there were two long narrow windows with small panes. The floor was stone paved and sprinkled with sand after cleaning to stop the stones being smeared with filth from the yard. There was a door off the passage that went into the dairy. Again there was a flagged floor and large bowls of cream waiting to go through the churn and through the wooden press, until it was made into butter. It was then put into small round containers, the lid put on and the Bowden Head rose decoration printed on it. There was a small sitting room which was only used on special occasions.

Across the road was a croft with the school buildings and teacher's cottage. After the school was closed and no teacher was needed, the two buildings were made into a house occupied by the Waterhouse family.

Mr. Waterhouse was a very good photographer and we were fortunate to have had him in the town. Almost every family had at one time or another had their children photographed by him. They are still shown proudly. I have two of my sister and myself. They are beautifully taken and as clear today as they were 80-odd years ago.

He was a very old man when he died and at the time of his funeral there had been a terrific snow storm. The funeral was at Chinley Chapel and it was impossible to bring horses and vehicles up the Wash Lane to Bowden Head. They decided the best thing to do would be to put the coffin on a sledge fastened by ropes, held by the bearers. This they did, but on the steep part of the lane the men lost control and the sledge went speeding off towards the Chapel. They caught up with it near the Wash!

Chapel Carnival in the park. The Rose Queen proudly leads the procession.

CHAPTER ~ 15 ~

SIGHTS AND SOUNDS OF WAKES WEEK

With the exception of Christmas, Chapel Wakes Week was the highlight of the year. All the works closed down and there was a holiday atmosphere in the town. Mothers made new clothes for themselves and their children and these were flaunted on every occasion. Special cakes were made and pieces of ham boiled in readiness for feeding the visiting relatives. Day trips were planned and for these fathers always wore their best suits and usually a bowler hat.

One of the favourite trips was to Haddon Hall. A train was taken to Bakewell and, after calling at a cafe for a Bakewell pudding and a cup of tea, we were on our way to Haddon. The Hall was unoccupied in those days and sparsely furnished. Even so, the beautiful and ancient building with so much atmosphere never lost its appeal. We could hardly wait to hear the romantic tale of Dorothy Vernon eloping with John Manners. We were all very quiet as we were shown the door and flight of steps down which they eloped, climbed onto their horses and fled away into the night.

Buxton, of course, was a must. We were always told to behave ourselves when we were there as, in those days Buxton was a truly snobbish place, especially in the gardens and pavilion. Buxton was famous as a Spa. Many rich people came to partake of the healing waters. They hired wheel chairs which were on display at the bottom of The Slopes. The wheelchairs were made of cane with a hood over the seat. There was a front cover and if the weather was cold or wet a glass window could be closed across to shield the occupant's face. A man could be hired to push the chair but many people had a private nurse and, if there was a young family, a governess as well.

Spring Gardens was elegant. The shops were high class and expensive. In front of each shop there was a veranda consisting of a wrought iron arched frame with a glass dome. Inside, the verandas were decorated with hanging baskets of flowers.

Milligan's was the only shop we went into. It was a ladies outfitters and sold materials. My mother used to buy printed Shantung silk for our best dresses and trimmings for hats. On entering the shop we were met by a man looking most elegant in full morning dress. He gave a slight bow then directed us to the department we wanted. He was called a shop walker and was only engaged by high class shops.

There was always a beautiful display of clothes but my attention was caught by the transferance of money from each counter to the office in the corner of the shop. On the ceiling above each counter and leading to and from the office, were fluted wire tracks. Attached to them were round wooden shuttle containers with an opening closed or opened by a spring latch. At one side was a short rope with a wooden handle. When pulled, this lowered the container and the assistant behind the counter could put in money. She then pulled another short rope which sent the shuttle on the ceiling line to the office. They put the change into the container and sent it back to the counter. This method of dealing with cash was a very modern invention in those days and used in all large shops.

In Chapel, when the fair arrived, there was great excitement. Crowds of children waited for a free ride on the Friday night when various attraction had been tested and all was ship-shape and ready for the Saturday rush. I can just remember the fair being in the Market Place but later it was moved to the field above the New Inn, next to the Slack's shed and near the Railway bridge. It became known as the fairground. The field also contained the Town Band room, a wooden hut heated by a coal stove. The band, which was officially formed in 1882, used this hut up until the 1980s. It then moved to the old scout hut on Eccles Road before the building of the new bandroom by the cricket field.

The fair was owned by a family called Hibbert. They were delightful people who had been coming to Chapel so many years they were known to almost everybody. They had a marvellous caravan and you were always welcome to drop in for a cup of tea.

It was a very good fair with plenty of rides and stalls to test your skills. The dobby horse roundabout of course was the favourite of adults as well as children. I remember that one year there was a cocks and hens roundabout as well. There were little gentle swing-boats for children and large heavy ones for groups of grown-ups.

There were various stalls, coconut shies and dart throwing and always popular with the men was rifle shooting. At some stalls you shot at rows of clay pipes but the favourite one was shooting at celluloid balls floating unevenly on jets of water. There were no prizes given at the shooting stalls. It was a matter of showing off your skill!

I remember once when I was growing up, shooting down eleven out of twelve of these balls which was an achievement. A tipsy voice from the crowd shouted: "Tom Nadin will never be dead whilst she is living". I felt very proud of this as Tom Nadin was my grandfather and was the champion shot of Derbyshire at one time. We still have cups he won more than 100 years ago.

Enjoying the Town Band in the park

Every Wakes Sunday the

Chapel Rose Queen, 1912. My sister Winnie is second from the left.

Vicar from the Church held a service in the fairground. There was always a large congregation with many people from the town attending. The Town Band played for the hymns. With the colour of the fair and so many people joining in the singing of the hymns, it was a very impressive service.

One other event that people looked forward to in Wakes Week was the cricket match between Dove Holes and Chapel. Dove Holes had a very good team and there was great rivalry between them. It was a great day. All the family used to come to watch the match. Every inch of the ground was filled. It was great for the children, and if bored by the match they could play in the fields around the ground. Special refreshments were put on including sherry trifle provided by Nobles, from the Kings Arms. During the match the music could be heard from the fair adding to the festive air.

CHAPTER

~ 16 ~

A MIDSUMMER DAY'S DREAM

On another special day of our Summer holiday we were told to play in the yard and keep off the road in expectation of a wonderful sight. This was the day the brewery horses that had been working in Stockport, being relieved of harness and trappings, were brought up to Chapel, then taken to land near Slack Hall Farm known locally as "Poor Piece". This was common land where cattle could be put out to lay and it was a haven where gypsies made camp. Here the gypsies lived in peace, making clothes pegs which they carried in baskets to sell from door to door. Also for a copper they would tell your fortune.

Slack Hall Farm.

As we waited with great excitement for the horses to put in an appearance, people carried out buckets of water and placed them in the gutter so that a few of the horses get a drink.

It was a spectacular sight as the horses came into view at the top of the hill. They moved towards us like something out of a dream. There were greys, blacks and chestnuts, all with long manes flying, floating in the air like wings. Road and pavements were packed with them. They moved towards us like a ballet. Everyone watched from their windows. It was a wonderful and rare sight. I think their shoes must have been removed as they passed so quietly, making it even more dream-like. How wonderful it must have been for them when they reached "Poor piece" and rolled on the soft turf and fed on the fresh green grass.

Across the road from Slack Hall Farm on the right hand side is a lane which runs parallel to the "Poor Piece". It leads to Stonyford and Bagshaw, then joins Peaslows. A lane leads from "Poor Piece" called Gypsy Lane and across the lane from it is a gate into a field called Bendigo Gate.

Towards the end of the last century, bare-fisted fighting was made illegal but illicit fighting continued secretly up and down the country. The last bare-fisted fight ever to be fought in England was reputed to be in Chapel and took place in the field called Bendigo Gate. On the day of the fight, Chapel was crowded with men on horseback and people on foot and in carriages all making their way to see the fight. Lots of gold sovereigns were wagered on the result of the fight. The field was named ever after "Bold Bendigo", the name of the man who won the fight.

Down the lane below Bendigo Gate there was a cottage where there lived a very strange character called Hannah Furness. Although she lived in such a remote place, she was well known in Chapel and often attended services in the Wesleyan Chapel. People always turned to look at her if only for her way of dressing. She always wore six petticoats, plus a skirt, three pairs of stockings, three pairs of mittens, two bonnets and a pair of men's boots. She was always late for the church service and disturbed the service as she clomped down the aisle. One Sunday she arrived as people were leaving after the service. When told that she was too late and that she should try to get there on time, she said that she never bothered with clocks. Her time was set by the sun and moon.

Bagshaw is a delightful little hamlet and seems to have changed little over the centuries. It is quiet and remote and one could hardly believe that it could ever become the centre of a great deal of attention. However, it became so because of a family called Shatwell who lived in a cottage witha small croft at the side. In this croft they kept, almost unbelievably, an animal which is rare enough in England - a bear. It was trained to dance and was known as Shotter's Dancing Bear. It became famous and was hired out to village fairs around the district. My father remembered seeing it dancing in Chapel Market Place.

One Summer night we were put to bed early and told that there would be a surprise next morning but we would have to get up early to see it. Just after dawn my mother woke us, wrapped us in warm shawls then sat us on the wide ledge of the window that faced up the street. We did not have long to wait before a lovely sight came into view, moving slowly down the hill towards us. It was a circus on its way to Sheffield. The caravans were painted in bright colours, some with flower motifs on the side. The performing horses were running freely filling the road and footpath. The drivers of the vans waved to us when they saw us in the window. We got more and more excited. Then a miracle seemed to happen, as from behind one of the vans there appeared the last thing we ever dreamed of seeing. An elephant, walking down Chapel main street! We dashed from window to window watching until it was out of sight. We were left speechless.

There was a sequel to this. That day my father was starting new work in Castleton. He hired Garlick's horse and dray to take equipment. As they went along Rushop Edge they saw that someone had removed coping stones from the wall and left them in the road. My father was furious to think that anyone could be so heartless as to leave such a dangerous trap for horses to stumble upon. He and the driver jumped off the dray to put them back onto the wall, only to find when they got to them that they were elephant droppings!

During the holidays we had lots of games to play. Hopscotch, marbles, whip and top were the favourites. We could all manage to make a whip with a stick and a piece of string. Every house seemed to have a top that had been handed down through the family. There were two kinds of top. A squat round one and one about two to three inches high shaped like the end of a carrot. It was called a monkey top and you had to be skilful to handle it as when hit it jumped into the air for a yard or two and it was difficult to catch up with it for the next swipe with the whip. Before playing, we put splotches of coloured chalks on them, then as they spun it made a perfect pattern.

We all had pieces of old clothes line for skipping ropes and we invented many variations of skipping. At times my father would lend us a long rope that stretched across the road. This was too heavy for us to turn but there were always volunteers from amongst the fathers. There was method in their madness! Before long mothers would come out to watch and, encouraged by the men, join in the skipping. This caused much fun and plenty of witty remarks and laughter.

On wet days my mother sometimes let us bring our friends to play in the house. I remember one day we played shop, selling clothes as this did not need much clearing away when we finished. We hung clothes on hooks round the room and hats and shoes on the piano. Quite large price tickets were pinned to the garments and hats. We took turns at being the shopkeeper. The following Saturday morning my father came dashing into the house to change into his best cap as he was going to the bank and it was almost closing time. When he returned my mother noticed that his cap still had our price ticket for 4s/6d pinned to the back, with a hat pin that had a large fancy knob on the end!

There were two other important days in the Summer, one dreaded and the other enjoyed. Blanket washing could be a nightmare if the weather was not good. All signs were observed such as "red sky at night, shepherds' delight, red sky in the morning, shepherds' warning". The most reliable one was to look where the cattle were grazing. If they were high up on the hills it was certain to be a fine day. It was very hard work, swishing heavy blankets about in the tub with a dolly peg then turning them several times through the mangle. This was repeated through several lots of rinsing water. Again, each rinsing had to go through the mangle. It was back aching and exhausting. When they were finally hanging out on the clothes line, there was a feeling of relief and pride at the sight of them blowing gently in the warm breeze.

Jam making was another special, very pleasant time. We were always willing to help by taking the stalks off the fruits or sorting out the softover-ripe ones which we were allowed to eat. We always managed to sneak some ripe ones without being caught. The heavy brass jam pan was lifted off the hook in the pantryceiling, filled with fruit and sugar with a small amount of water, put on the gas stove and brought to a steady boil. There was a delicious smell in the kitchen. When ready, it was cooled off and put into pottery jars. No glass jars were used in my young days. Jam making went on for several weeks as different fruit ripened. Strawberries, gooseberries and rhubarb from the garden. Rhubarb jam was one of my favourites as my mother used to flavour it with stem ginger. Apricots and raspberries were bought from the shops but there was always a pleasant trip down to Bridgeholme Green at the bottom of Charley Lane, where the farm had an orchard. They sold plums and damsons.

In the Spring when Seville oranges came into the shops, there were days of making marmalade. This was a very different procedure. The peel was sliced very thinly and left to soak with the pips for 24 hours before being boiled with the sugar.

It was a most satisfying sight to see all the shelves in the kitchen cupboard filled with pots of jam, marmalade and apple jelly.

When the First World War was declared Chapel's Volunteers were called to arms. Top: Recruits leaving Chapel Station in September 1914. Below: This group was photographed in February, 1915.

CHAPTER ~ 17 ~

THE BEGINNING OF THE END

There was a company of Volunteer soldiers in Chapel who trained hard in the Drill Hall on Market Street and on the shooting range in the Target field. The Drill Hall was situated at what is now the intersection of Thornbrook Road, near the Health Centre. It was a big corrugated iron building and dances were sometimes held there.

When the First World War was declared the Volunteers were called to arms. Those who were fit enough went for training and then to the war zone. It was when news began to come through of boys being killed or wounded that gloom set in over the town. The boy I mentioned at the beginning of my story, called Erbie Ford was one of the first to be killed. His family were devastated as were all who knew him. Households dreaded the sight of the telegraph boy cycling along on his rounds, fearing that he might stop at their house with a telegram containing bad news.

Older men were soon called up to serve which caused distress as most of them were fathers of large families. Although my father volunteered many times he was always turned down as unfit, which upset him as he felt he should have been serving with his friends.

The uniform the soldiers wore was anything but smart. It was made from rough khaki coloured material. With it they wore heavy boots with puttees wrapped around their legs up to the knee. They carried a heavy gun with a bayonet fastened to the side and a steel helmet strapped to their backs.

The fighting in France was horrific. Mostly hand-to-hand with bayonets drawn. Soldiers dug deep trenches for protection in Winter weather they fought knee-deep in mud. Flanders mud was the topic of conversation and even used in songs of the war. It must have been a nightmare as the guns were pulled by teams of horses floundering through the mud.

Hundreds of horses were killed. Soon there was a shortage of horses and the Government started to commandeer as many as possible. Even farmers had to part with them. This made it hard work as many had their sons in the forces.

In 1916 the Government formed the Woman's Land Army, made up of young women from the towns who were fit enough to do a man's work on the farm. They were dressed in a slouch hat, khaki coat and shirt and knee breeches. This was a complete innovation as women had never worn trousers before! Thick woollen socks and heavy boots completed the outfit. They soon settled on the farms and learned to handle animals and farm equipment competently.

As the war went on, it became more and more mechanised. Women began to do work that at one time would only have been done by men. They were employed in munitions factories and on the railways. Women worked as postmen, also lamplighters, using a hook on the end of the long pole to light and then next morning to extinguish them.

Mrs. Spencer, who lived in Frith Knoll, a large house on Eccles Road, opened it as a convalescent home for soldiers who were recuperating from war wounds. With its lovely gardens it was an ideal place for these badly wounded men to recover and regain their confidence.

Mr. Herbert Frood started a small factory in the old fustian mill making brake linings. This occupied many Chapel girls and eventually several of them were driving lorries for him.

German prisoners of war were sent to England. Some came to Chapel and were lodged at Bank Hall. They were put to work on farms and at any job that was too heavy for women. They were a help in the War Effort and possibly glad to have some freedom.

It was wonderful the day that we heard the war was over and that we were the victors. There were colourful celebrations and the church bells were rung. Yet there was sadness and heartache for so many families. Gradually, the demobbed soldiers came home. There was a great welcome for them, but they looked tired and shocked by their experiences. Those who did not return were commemorated at the Memorial in the Market Place. Four Chapel soldiers were awarded the Distinguished Conduct Medal (D.C.M.). They were Frank Longson, Arthur Barlow, Jimmy Heyworth and Fred Wilshaw. When the new Warmbrook Estate was built after the war, streets were named after them.

It was difficult for returning soldiers to re-start their lives but, as time went on, the old community spirit began to emerge in the town. Cricket and football matches were played again. Churches had their sermons parades, the band played at all the functions. A number of returning soldiers formed the Chapel Male Voice Choir which still flourishes today.

Once again Christmas was enjoyed by the children. Life returned to a measure of normality after the War, though it was never to be quite the same again. Twenty years later it was plunged into turmoil once more during the Second World War of 1939-45. Even so, as the town's children grew up they carried on the traditions that had made Chapel-en-le-Frith a very special place with its warm-hearted people and beautiful countryside.

Index

Appleton, Mrs....61
Anderson, Mrs....51
ARP services....20
Bagshaw....135
Bakewell workhouse....21
Bakewell....130
Barber, John....127
Barlow, Arthur....30, 142
Barlow's farm, haymaking....***43***
Barlow, Walter....21, ***23***
Barlows, The, publicans....96
Barmoor Clough....49
Beard, Raymond, Jacob, Jim and Joe....62
Beardwood, Mr....30
Bee Hive, Inn....***86***
Bendigo Gate....135
Bendigo Bold....135
Bennet, Reuben....27
Bennett, The Rev Norman....97
Berrisford, Jodie....***23***
Bishop's Blaze Inn....***93,*** 94
Blouse works....123
Bonfire night....97, ***97***
Boswell, Mrs....61
Bowden Hall....10
Bowden Head farm..23, 27, 125, 127, 128
Bowden Lane....123
Bramwell Frank....61
Bramwell, Arthur....83
Bramwell, Mrs....31
Brewery....37, 38, 65, ***66, 68***
Bridgeholme Green....138
Brocklehurst, Miss....83
Brunt, Maggie, Polly and Ann....31, 33
Bugsworth Basin....121
Bull's Head Inn....***93,*** 94
Burrfields....63
Buxton....130
Carrington's shop....65
Carrington, H....***53***
Castleton Road....127
Cattle market....23, 96
Cavendish Girls' High School....108
Chapel Carnival....129
Chapel Central Station....54, ***55***
Chapel Male Voice Choir....142
Chapel Milton....***120,*** 121, ***122, 124***
Chapel Town Band....131, ***132***
Chapel Wakes Week....130
Charity scholarship Dixen and Kirk....108
Charley Lane....138
Chesnut House....51
Chesnut trees....***50***
Chinley....126
Chinley Chapel....128
Church Brow....85, ***93,*** 94, 101, ***102***
Church gennel....***93***
Clara, cousin....27, 127
Combs Moss....83
Combs lake....111
Constitutional Hall....114
Co-op....63
Cooper's coalyard....51
Cornheys Farm....126
Cottrill, F....***53***
Council, The....10, 12, 14
Court days....14
Cowburn Tunnel....126
Cricket, Chapel Ladies team....***82***
Cricket Club....83, ***84***
Cromwell House....63
Cross Keys Inn....***122,*** 124
Crossings Road....117
Curfew bell....35
Dawe, Mr, stationmaster....21, 103
Derby County Football Club....54
Dog Inn....60, 61
Donkey stone....29
Dove Holes quarry....10, 18, 67, 121
Dove Holes tunnel....18
Down Lee farm....23
Drill Hall....8, 140
Drum and Monkey Inn....123
Eaton, Ben, cobbler....59
Eaves Farm....30
Eaves Hall....41
Eccles Road....***93,*** 114
Fergusson, Robert....57
First World War...8, 49, 65, 105, ***139,*** 140
Ferodo Ltd....***9***
Football club....113
Ford, Erbie....7, 89, 140
Ford Hall....10
Ford, Mam, Dad, Ernest, Sally, Herbert....88,89,90,91,92
Ford, Miss, teacher....105
Ford, Teddy....101
Frith, Mrs....104
Frood, Herbert....9
Freemasons....91
Furness, Hannah....135
Garlick, John Arthur....18, 24
Garlick's stables....85
Gas works....10
Gipsy Lane....135
Greyhound Inn....***93,*** 94
Goddard, Miss....***58***
Gorsty Low....***122***
Haddon Hall....130
Hallam, Mr....30
Hamer, Mr....94
Hayfield Road....115, 118, 121
Health Centre....140
Hearse House (The Heritage Centre)....***13***
Heyworth Jimmy....142
Hibbert, Billy....35, 98
Hibbert's fair....131
Hickey, William *The Daily Express*....54
High Street....63, ***93,*** 96
Hill, Valerie....6
Hollies, The....56
Hospital, Fever (now High Peak Borough Council offices)....115
Humphrey, Uncle....127
Hyde, Miss....63
Hyde, Joseph and Ebenezer....101
Ibbotson's Engineering Works...10, 31, 63
Ibbotson, J....***53***
Ibbotson, S....***53***
Isaac, cousin....127
Kelly, John's joinery workshop....22
Kerr, Mr and Mrs....41
King's Arms Inn....***93,*** 96, 114, 133
Kirk, T....***53***
Kirk, Mrs....60
Leckenby, Mr, plumber....101
Lee Sammy....42, 63
Lingards....10
Lizzie, cousin....127
Livesley, Alfie....46
Lomas, Nicholas and Nall....65
Lomas, Alf....83
Long, Parmainus....42

Index

Longson, Colin ***47***
Longson's farm 18, 39,45, 109
Longson, Frank, Matthew, Norman ***53,*** 142
Longson, Matthew foundry 39
Longson, Sam......................46,***48,*** 52, 103
Longson, Tom.....21, 22, ***23,*** 39, 40, ***47, 53***
Lower Courses farm..............................23
Lower Eaves 41
Lyal, Kathleen and David.......................44
Malcoff 127
Manchester Guardian, The 57
Manners, John 130
Marchington, A ***53***
Marchington, Ann 7
Marchington, J.......................................***53***
Market Place
25,26,27,***28,***35,***93,***104,***95,***96,***97,***97 99, 142
Market Street
8, ***11,*** 59, 63, 65, ***93, 112,113,*** 140
Marsh, Mrs, chip shop 83
Marshall, butchers 101
Memorial Park..34
Memorial Institute 65
Methodist Manse 63
Memorial, Market Place.......................142
Meyer, Teddie, barber 60
Middleton, Miss, teacher......................105
Milligan's, Buxton 131
Mitchell's smallholding 63
Muir, J..***53***
Muir, Paddy.....................................18,24
Nadin, Isaac ***23***
Nadin, Tom, grandfather 132
Nannies well..117
Nall, George 114
Needham, Samuel Mr and Mrs 41
Needham, Wilfred ***53***
New Inn...................................51, 131
New Mills Secondary School 108
New Smithy 94, 126
New Year's Eve......................................34
Noble, family 103, 133
Noble, Johnnie and Bobbie..................114
Oatcakes 30
Parish Church, St Thomas Becket.....49, ***93***
Parish Church bellringers ***34***
Park farm...21
Park fields 39, 42
Park Road ...15, 40, ***36,*** 37, 39, 65, 92, 117
Partington, Mr, solicitor..........................40
Partridge, Mr, greengrocer 27, 101
Peak Dale quarry 10
Pearce, Harold 100
Peaslows 135
Pell, Mr and Mrs....................................91
Peter, Uncle 85
Pinder, P...***53***
Pink, Mr and Mrs George 51, 99
Pink, Mary and Connie 99
Plumpton Farm, Bagshaw 89
Poor Piece 135
Potts, joiner 101
Primitive Methodist Chapel 22, 49
Rag mill 123
Railway station, North West..................***19***
Ridge Hall...10
Roebuck, The Inn...........................***93,*** 97
Rose Queen...............................129, ***133***
Rowtan Road 6
Royal Oak Inn 58
Rushop Edge..136
Second World War.......................20, 142
Shatwell family 136
Sherwood Foresters, 6th Battalion...........92
Shire Oaks 127
Shirt works 10
Shotter's dancing bear 136
Shrove Tuesday 35
Sidebotham, B ***53***
Sidebotham, E ***53***
Sidebotham, John ***56***
Simpson's Butcher's shop ***32***
Simpson, Mr Sam, brewer ....
38,***64,*** 65, 67, 69, 97
Simpson, Miss Nellie 59
Slack, Ada and George......................91, 92
Slack,Freddy, Herbert 99, 131
Slack Hall farm 20,21, ***134,*** 135
Slack, Sam 18, 24
Smith Brook 31
Smith, Jonathan 20, 21
Smithfield wadding works................10, 42
South Head 83
Sparrow Pit..20
Stables, Mr and Mrs 40
Stancliffe Brothers, brewery ***66***
Standfast, Rev ***53***
Stanley House 101
Station road 20
Stewart, Dorothy 7
Stocks, The..96
Stoddart 121
Streader, Mrs 31
Stoneyford 135
Swan Inn ***93,*** 96
Target field.................44, 92, 93, 109, 140
Taylor, George's milk float ***13***
Taylor, Mr....................................30, 110
Terrace Road................................94, 101
The Wash ***125,*** 126
Thornbrook Road 8, 140
Top o'th' Plane.....................................121
Town Crier 33
Town Hall..14
Town End 51, 63, ***77,*** 104
Town End Foundry..................................9
Town End Garage 54
Tunstead Milton 49
Turner, A ***53***
Upper Eaves 41
Vernon, Dorothy 130
Viaducts, Chapel Milton ***124***
Vicarage..51
Wakes week...............................100, 131
Walker, Mr....................................18, 38
Walton's grocery....................................***14***
War Memorial 26, 96, 114
Warming stone 7, 37, 40
Warmbrook estate................................142
Waterhouse, Mr, photographer 128
Wesleyan School 20
Wesleyan Chapel 49
Whaley Bridge.......................................49
Whitehough 20
Wilkie, Miss, teacher 105
Williams, Billy 89
Wilshaw, Fred 142
Winnie, sister................7, 37, 67, 104, ***133***
Winterbottom, farmer..........................123
Woodcock family 101
Work House...87
Working Week, The............70, ***73, 76, 80***

THE WARMING STONE
W.H. MARSHALL